Pastor Michelle Caba—

W9-BYF-940

SELF STUDY

BIBLE

COURSE

BY DEREK PRINCE

WHITAKER
HOUSE

All Scripture quotations are taken from the King James Version
of the Holy Bible.

The books *Laying on of Hands, Foundation for Faith, From Jordan to Pentecost,*
and *Resurrection of the Dead,* which Derek Prince refers to in the *Self Study Bible
Course,* are now published in *The Spirit-Filled Believer's Handbook,* © 1993 by
Derek Prince Ministries—International, published by Creation House. Please
refer to this *Handbook* for further information regarding these titles.

SELF STUDY BIBLE COURSE

Derek Prince Ministries—International
P.O. Box 19501
Charlotte, NC 28219
www.dpmusa.org

ISBN: 0-88368-421-7
Printed in the United States of America
© 1969 by Derek Prince Ministries—International

Whitaker House
30 Hunt Valley Circle
New Kensington, PA 15068
www.whitakerhouse.com

No part of this book may be reproduced or transmitted in any form or
by any means, electronic or mechanical, including photocopying,
recording, or by any information storage and retrieval system,
without permission in writing from the publisher.

6 7 8 9 10 11 12 13 14 15 16 ⊔⊔ 12 11 10 09 08 07 06 05 04

CONTENTS

SELF STUDY BIBLE COURSE

BY DEREK PRINCE

INTRODUCTION: INSTRUCTIONS TO THE STUDENT

Read these Instructions before answering any questions!

Almost anywhere in the world today where Christianity has come, we find some people who would like to be Christians—but they are weak, fearful, discouraged, defeated. In almost every case the reason is the same: such people have never learned to study the Bible for themselves and to apply its teaching in a practical way to their lives. That is why God says, in Hosea 4:6, "My people are destroyed for lack of knowledge." Once a person comes to know the truths of the Bible, and how to apply those truths in a practical way to his own life, the result is always the same: peace, victory, success, fruitfulness.

1. PURPOSE OF THIS BIBLE COURSE

This Self Study Course has four main aims:

(1) To provide you with a foundation of Bible knowledge on which you will be able to build a strong and successful Christian life;

(2) To give you practice in searching the scriptures, and in finding and claiming God's wonderful promises for yourself;

(3) To train you in analysing a passage of scripture so as to find out for yourself its correct meaning;

(4) To form in you the habit of accepting only those teachings about spiritual things which can be proved by direct reference to the Bible.

2. SYSTEM OF BIBLE REFERENCES

The translation of the Bible used throughout this Course is the King James ("Authorised") Version. This is the version most familiar and most easily available to English speaking people all over the world. However, the great truths of scripture taught in this Course do not depend upon any one particular version, but would be equally clear in any other reliable version.

You must learn where to find each Book in the Bible, and to understand the system of abbreviating the names of the Books which is used throughout the Course (for a detailed key to this system, see the "KEY TO ABBREVIATED NAMES OF BIBLE BOOKS" on page 5). References to passages of scripture are given as follows: first, the Book; second, the chapter; third, the verse. For example, Rom. 3:23 indicates the Epistle to the Romans, chapter 3, verse 23. Again, I John 2:14 indicates the First Epistle of John, chapter 2, verse 14. In Books which have no chapters, the verse number immediately follows the Book. For example, 3 John 2 indicates the Third Epistle of John, verse 2.

3. HOW TO DO THE STUDIES

At the top of each question paper there is a short paragraph, headed "INTRODUCTION". This gives a brief summary of the main teaching contained in the questions that follow. Always read through the "INTRODUCTION" carefully, before attempting to answer the questions.

In the first question paper, "STUDY NO. 1: GOD'S PLAN OF SALVATION", there are 22 questions. In parenthesis, after each question, there are references to one or more passages of scripture. The answer to each question is always to be found in the passages referred to in the parenthesis after that question. Following after each question, there is a space, indicated by one or more dotted lines, in which you must write your answer to the question. The correct procedure for answering the questions is as follows:

(1) Read the question carefully.

(2) Find the scripture passages referred to in parenthesis and read through these passages carefully, until you find the answer to that question.

(3) In the space indicated by the dotted lines, write down in brief simple language the answer which you have found.

Sometimes the answer to one question must be divided up into two or more parts. In such cases, the spaces for each part of the answer are numbered (1) .... (2) .... (3) .... etc., and each part of the answer must be written in the correct numbered space.

To make all this quite plain, we give you here the first two questions of Study No. 1, with the correct answers written in, to show you how and where to write your answers:

1. For what purpose were all things created? (Rev. 4:11)

   For God's pleasure

   ....

2. Write down 3 things which God is worthy to receive (Rev. 4:11)

   Glory   Honour   Power

   (1) .... (2) .... (3) ....

When doing these questions for yourself, do not merely write down the answers given above. First, look up the scripture passages for yourself, and work out your own answers. Then check your answers with the ones given above, to see if they are correct. Then carry on answering the rest of the questions in the same way, until you have completed the whole Study.

4. MEMORY WORK

At the beginning of each question paper, there is a passage given for memory work. You must learn this passage by heart. This is how to proceed:-

Take a blank card and on one side neatly print the Study number in the top left-hand corner, and then the scripture reference in the middle, followed by the Study title. Here is how your first card should look, for example:-

> Study No. 1
>
> ROM. 6:23
>
> God's Plan of Salvation (1)

Then, on the other side of the card, neatly write the scripture passage itself, as follows:-

> "For the wages of sin is
> death; but the gift of God
> is eternal life through
> Jesus Christ our Lord."

Carry your memory cards with you. Whenever you have a spare moment during the day, take the opportunity of reviewing your memory verses. Regular review is the secret of successful memory work. In this way you will not only learn the Word by heart, but the Word will be in your heart, giving you guidance, strength, spiritual food, victory over the devil, and seed to sow in the hearts of others.

When repeating the passage to be memorised, always begin and end by saying the reference to the Book, chapter, and verse. For instance, the first memory passage should be repeated as follows:-"Romans six, twenty three. For the wages of sin is death; but the gift of God is eternal life through Jesus Christ our Lord. Romans six, twenty three." In this way you will not only memorise the passage but also its reference in the Bible. Thus you will be able to find it easily at any time, whether for yourself or others.

5. PROCEDURE FOR WORKING THROUGH THE COURSE

Write in your answer to every question in Study No. 1, and then—with your Bible closed—write out the memory work in the space provided at the end. Then turn over the page to the Correct Answers to this Study. Check your own answers by reference to these Correct Answers. If in any case your answer does not agree with the corresponding Correct Answer, read through both the question and the relevant scripture passage again, until you understand clearly the reason for the Correct Answer.

On the page opposite the Correct Answers you will find Notes on these Answers, which explain them more fully. Take time to read through these Notes, and to look up any further passages of scripture referred to in them.

Finally, evaluate your own work by writing against each answer that you have given the mark that you feel you deserve for that answer. A simple standard of marking is given together with the Correct Answers. If an answer is valued at more than one mark, do not allow yourself the full mark, unless your answer is as complete as the Correct Answer. Remember that the marks for the memory work are important!

Add up your marks for Study No. 1, and check this total by reference to the three standards given at the bottom of the Correct Answers. 50% or over rates as a "Pass"; 70% or over as a "Credit"; 80% or over as a "Distinction".

When you have completed all that there is to do in connection with Study No. 1, turn over to Study No. 2, and work through this in the same way. Continue like this until you have completed the whole Course. The methods for doing the last two Studies—Nos. 13 and 14—are slightly different, but they are clearly explained at the head of each Study.

Remember! You must NEVER turn over to the Correct Answers for any Study until you have first written in your own answer to every question in that Study—including the memory work!

When you have completed the last Study, turn over to the page headed "MARKS FOR THE COURSE". Write in your marks for each Study in the space provided, add them up, and evaluate your standard of achievement for the Course as a whole. However, you will find that the final evaluation cannot be expressed merely in terms of "marks", but only in terms of enduring spiritual blessings and achievements which will have come to you through faithfully working through the complete Course.

6. FINAL PERSONAL ADVICE

(1) Begin each Study with prayer, asking God to guide you and give you understanding.

(2) Do not work too quickly. Do not try to accomplish the whole Study at one sitting. Read through each passage of scripture several times, until you are sure of its meaning. It will often be helpful to read several verses before or after the actual passage, in order to grasp its full meaning.

(3) Write neatly and clearly. Do not make your answers longer than necessary. Use a well sharpened pencil, or a ball point pen.

(4) Pay special attention to the memory work.

(5) Pray daily that God may help you to apply in your own life the truths that you are learning.

KEY TO ABBREVIATED NAMES OF BIBLE BOOKS
BOOKS OF OLD TESTAMENT

I THE LAW

Genesis	- Gen.
Exodus	- Ex.
Leviticus	- Lev.
Numbers	- Num.
Deuteronomy	- Deut.

II HISTORY

Joshua	- Josh.
Judges	- Jud.
Ruth	- Ruth
1 Samuel	- 1 Sam.
2 Samuel	- 2 Sam.
1 Kings	- 1 Kin.
2 Kings	- 2 Kin.
1 Chronicles	- 1 Chron.
2 Chronicles	- 2 Chron
Ezra	- Ezra
Nehemiah	- Neh.
Esther	- Est.

III POETICAL BOOKS

Job	- Job
Psalms	- Psa.
Proverbs	- Prov.

Ecclesiastes	- Ecc.
Song of Solomon	- Song

IV MAJOR PROPHETS

Isaiah	- Is.
Jeremiah	- Jer.
Lamentations	- Lam.
Ezekiel	- Ezek.
Daniel	- Dan.

V MINOR PROPHETS

Hosea	- Hos.
Joel	- Joel
Amos	- Am.
Obadiah	- Ob.
Jonah	- Jon.
Micah	- Mic.
Nahum	- Nah.
Habbakuk	- Hab.
Zephaniah	- Zeph.
Haggai	- Hag.
Zechariah	- Zec.
Malachi	- Mal.

BOOKS OF NEW TESTAMENT

I GOSPELS

Matthew	- Matt.
Mark	- Mark
Luke	- Luke
John	- John

II HISTORY

The Acts	- Acts

III PAULINE EPISTLES

Romans	- Rom.
I Corinthians	- 1 Cor.
2 Corinthians	- 2 Cor.
Galatians	- Gal.
Ephesians	- Eph.
Philippians	- Phil.
Colossians	- Col.
I Thessalonians	- 1 Thes.

2 Thessalonians	- 2 Thes.
I Timothy	- 1 Tim.
2 Timothy	- 2 Tim.
Titus	- Tit.
Philemon	- Philem.
Hebrews	- Heb.

IV GENERAL EPISTLES

James	- Jam.
1 Peter	- 1 Pet.
2 Peter	- 2 Pet.
1 John	- 1 John
2 John	- 2 John
3 John	- 3 John
Jude	- Jude

V PROPHECY

Revelation	- Rev.

(Note that "John" stands for the Gospel of John, but "1 John" for the First Epistle of John, and so on.)

STUDY NO. 1
GOD'S PLAN OF SALVATION

Introduction:

Sin is an inward spiritual attitude of rebellion towards God, which is expressed in outward acts of disobedience. We are all sinners in this way, and by our sinful lives we rob God of the glory due to Him. Sin is followed by three main consequences: first, inward spiritual death, or alienation from God; second, the physical death of the body; third, final and eternal banishment from the presence of God to a place of darkness and torment. Christ came to save us from our sins. Himself without sin, He took our sins upon Him, died in our place, and rose again from the dead, that we might be forgiven and receive eternal life.

Memory work: Rom. 6:23   Please check when Memory card prepared ☐

A. SIN AND ITS CONSEQUENCES   *Part A – March 11th*

1. For what purpose were all things created? (Rev. 4:11)

   ....

2. Write down 3 things which God is worthy to receive (Rev. 4:11)

   (1) .... (2) .... (3) ....

3. In what way have all men sinned? (Rom. 3:23)

   ....

4. When men turned away from God, what were the first two sins that they committed? (Rom. 1:21)

   (1) ....

   (2) ....

5. What were the results of this? (Rom. 1:21)

   (1) In man's mind? ....

   (2) In man's heart? ....

6. Write down two facts about the human heart (Jer. 17:9)

   (1) ....

   (2) ....

7. Who alone knows the truth about the human heart? (Jer. 17:10)

   ....

8. Write down 13 evil things which come out of the human heart (Mark 7:21, 22)

   (1) .... (2) ....

   (3) .... (4) ....

   (5) .... (6) ....

   (7) .... (8) ....

   (9) .... (10) ....

   (11) .... (12) ....

   (13) ....

9. If we are able to do something good, and we do not do it, what does **God** call that? (Jam. 4:17)

   ....

10. If we say we have no sin, what are we doing to ourselves? (1 John 1:8)

....

11. If we say that we have not sinned, what are we doing to God? (1 John 1:10)

....

12. What consequence has sin brought upon all men? (Rom. 5:12; 6:23 Jam. 1:15)

....

13. What is the final end of all unrepentant sinners? (Matt. 25:41 Rev. 20:12-15)

....

14. Write down eight different kinds of people who will go to the lake of fire (Rev. 21:8)

(1) .... (2) ....

(3) .... (4) ....

(5) .... (6) ....

(7) .... (8) ....

B. THE PURPOSE OF CHRIST'S DEATH AND RESURRECTION — Part B - El April 1st

15. For what purpose did Christ come into the world? (1 Tim. 1:15)

....

16. Whom did Christ call, and whom did He receive? (Matt. 9:13 Luke 15:2)

....

17. Did Christ Himself commit any sins? (Heb. 4:15 1 Pet. 2:22)

....

18. What did Christ bear for us on the cross? (1 Pet. 2:24)

....

19. For what purpose did Christ die on the cross? (1 Pet. 3:18)

....

20. What 3 facts about Christ did Paul teach as the gospel? (1 Cor. 15:3, 4)

(1) ....

(2) ....

(3) ....

21. Seeing that Christ is now alive evermore, what is He able to do for those who come to Him? (Heb. 7:25)

....

22. Write down 3 things now offered to all men in the name of Jesus (Luke 24:47 Acts 4:12)

(1) ....

(2) ....

(3) ....

Memory work: Rom. 6:23 — Due March 18th in S.S.
Write out this verse from memory

....

....

....

DO NOT TURN THIS PAGE UNTIL YOU HAVE COMPLETED ALL ANSWERS IN THIS STUDY

STUDY NO. 1: GOD'S PLAN OF SALVATION

CORRECT ANSWERS AND MARKS

Question No.	Answers	Marks
1.	For God's pleasure	1
2.	(1) Glory (2) Honour (3) Power	3
3.	All have come short of the glory of God	1
4.	(1) They did not glorify God (2) They were not thankful	2
5.	(1) They became vain in their imaginations	1
	(2) Their foolish heart was darkened	1
6.	(1) It is deceitful above all things	1
	(2) It is desperately wicked	1
7.	The Lord (God)	1
8.	(1) Evil thoughts (2) Adulteries (3) Fornications	3
	(4) Murders (5) Thefts (6) Covetousness	3
	(7) Wickedness (8) Deceit (9) Lasciviousness	3
	(10) An evil eye (11) Blasphemy (12) Pride	3
	(13) Foolishness	1
9.	God calls that Sin	1
10.	We are deceiving ourselves	1
11.	We are making God a liar	1
12.	Death	1
13.	Everlasting fire — the lake of fire — the second death	1
14.	(1) The fearful (2) The unbelieving	2
	(3) The abominable (4) Muderers (5) Whoremongers	3
	(6) Sorcerers (7) Idolaters (8) All liars	3
15.	To save sinners	1
16.	Christ called and received sinners	1
17.	None	1
18.	Our sins	1
19.	To bring us to God	1
20.	(1) Christ died for our sins (2) He was buried	2
	(3) He rose again the third day	1
21.	To save them to the uttermost	1
22.	(1) Repentance (2) Remission of sins (3) Salvation	3

Consult Bible for Written Memory Work

If word perfect, 4 marks		4
(1 mark off for each mistake. If more than 3 mistakes, no marks)		—
	TOTAL	54

50% — 27   70% — 38   80% — 43

STUDY NO. 1: GOD'S PLAN OF SALVATION

NOTES ON CORRECT ANSWERS

(The numbers in the lefthand margin correspond to the numbers of the correct answers on the previous page)

1-4. Basically, man's sin is his failure to fulfill his God-given function. Man was created to glorify God. "He is the image and glory of God" (1 Cor. 11:7). Any behaviour of man that fails to glorify God is sinful.

3. "Come short of the glory of God." The picture is taken from an arrow shot at a mark, but falling short of it. The "mark" of man's existence is "the glory of God." But all have fallen short of this mark. (Compare Phil. 3:14.)

6-8. All these scriptures speak about "the heart" generally. They describe the inward condition of all fallen humanity, without any exceptions.

8. Not all these sins here mentioned are actually committed by all men. But the "seeds" of all these sins are found in every heart. Character and circumstances, combined, decide which of these "seeds" will actually bring forth the corresponding actions in any individual life.

9. Many people are guilty not so much for what they "commit" as for what they "omit". In Matt. 25:3, 25, 45, the foolish virgins, the unfaithful steward, and the "goat" nations are all condemned for what they did not do.

13. We must distinguish 2 different places: (1) "Hell" (Hebrew "sheol"; Greek "hades"): a place of confinement for departed souls, prior to resurrection and judgment (Luke 16:23). (2) "Gehenna" or "the lake of fire": a place of final, unending punishment for the wicked, after resurrection and judgment (Rev. 20:12-15).

14. Note the first 2 classes of the condemned: the "fearful" and the "unbelieving." How many "religious" people are included?

18. "Now once in the end of the world hath he (Christ) appeared to put away sin by the sacrifice of himself" (Heb. 9:26). By the sacrifices of the law of Moses sin was temporarily "covered" (See Heb. 10:1-4). By the death of Christ sin was finally "put away" (See Heb. 10:11-18).

19. Unforgiven sin is the great barrier between God and man (Is. 59:2). When sin was put away by Christ on the cross, the way was opened for man to come back to God. Any barriers that now remain are on man's side, not on God's.

20. "Faith" is built on "fact". The "gospel" is based on these 3 simple, historical facts.

21. "To the uttermost" includes every need of every sinner in time and eternity. Christ is sufficient for all.

STUDY NO. 2

GOD'S PLAN OF SALVATION
(Continued)

Introduction:

God now offers salvation to us not through any religion or good works, but through our personal faith in Christ. In order to be saved, we must acknowledge our sins and repent (that is, turn from our sins); we must believe that Christ died for us, and rose again; we must receive the risen Christ by faith as our personal Saviour, and we must publicly confess Him as our Lord. After we have received Christ in this way, He dwells continually in our hearts by faith, and He gives us eternal life and the power to lead a life of righteousness and victory over sin.

Memory work: John 1:12, 13 Please check when Memory card prepared ☐

(Review daily Romans 6:23)

C. HOW WE MAY RECEIVE SALVATION

23. When should we seek salvation? (Prov. 27:1 2 Cor. 6:2)

....

24. Can we save ourselves by our own good works? (Eph. 2:8, 9 Tit. 3:5)

....

25. Can we be saved by keeping the law? (Rom. 3:20)

....

26. If we desire God's mercy, what 2 things must we do? (Prov. 28:13)

(1) ....

(2) ....

27. If we confess our sins, what 2 things will God do for us? (1 John 1:9)

(1) ....

(2) ....

28. What is God's remedy to cleanse our hearts from all sin? (1 John 1:7)

....

29. If we desire to be saved, what 2 things must we do? (Rom. 10:9, 10)

(1) With our hearts? ....

....

(2) With our mouths? ....

....

30. If we come to Christ will He reject us? (John 6:37)

....

31. If we open our hearts to receive Christ, what promise has He given us? (Rev. 3:20)

....

32. If we receive Christ, what does He give us? (John 1:12)

....

33. What experience do we have as a result? (John 1:13)

....

34. When we receive Christ, what does God give us through Him? (Rom. 6:23)

....

35. Is it possible for us to know that we have eternal life? (1 John 5:13)

....

36. What record does God give us concerning Christ? (1 John 5:11)

....

37. If we have received Jesus Christ, the Son of God, what do we have? (1 John 5:12)

....

D. SALVATION GIVES POWER TO OVERCOME THE WORLD AND THE DEVIL —

3. 38. After we have received Christ, who lives in our hearts by faith? (Gal. 2:20 Eph. 3:17)

....

1. 39. What can we do through the strength which Christ gives us? (Phil. 4:13)

....

6. 40. If we confess Christ before men, what will He do for us? (Matt. 10:32)

....

....

2. 41. If we deny Christ before men, what will He do for us? (Matt. 10:33)

....

....

7. 42. What kind of person is able to overcome the world and its temptations?
(1) (1 John 5:4) ....
(2) (1 John 5:5) ....

4. 43. Why are God's children able to overcome the world? (1 John 4:4)

....

....

8. 44. By what 2 things do the people of God overcome the devil? (Rev. 12:11)
(1) ....
(2) ....

5. 45. Whom has God promised to receive to heaven as His child? (Rev. 21:7)

....

Memory work: John 1:12, 13
Write out these verses from memory. Primary Sunday

....

....

....

....

....

....

DO NOT TURN THIS PAGE UNTIL YOU HAVE COMPLETED ALL ANSWERS IN THIS STUDY

STUDY NO. 2: GOD'S PLAN OF SALVATION

(Continued)

CORRECT ANSWERS AND MARKS

Question No.	Answers	Marks
23.	Now, today	1
24.	No	1
25.	No	1
26.	(1) Confess our sins (2) Forsake our sins	2
27.	(1) Forgive us our sins	1
	(2) Cleanse us from all unrighteousness	1
28.	The blood of Jesus Christ, God's Son	1
29.	(1) Believe that God has raised Jesus from the dead	2
	(2) Confess Jesus as Lord	1
30.	No	1
31.	"I will come in"	1
32.	Power to become the sons of God	1
33.	We are born of God (= born again)	1
34.	Eternal life	1
35.	Yes (John wrote for that purpose)	1
36.	God has given us eternal life in Christ	2
37.	Eternal life	1
38.	Christ lives in our hearts	1
39.	All things (that God wishes us to do)	1
40.	He will confess us before His heavenly Father	1
41.	He will deny us before His heavenly Father	1
42.	(1) The one who is born of God (through his faith)	2
	(2) The one who believes that Jesus is the Son of God	1
43.	Because the one in them (= God) is greater than the one in the world (= the devil)	2
44.	(1) By the blood of the Lamb (= Christ)	1
	(2) By the word of their testimony	1
45.	Him that overcometh	1

Consult Bible for Written Memory Work

If word perfect, 4 marks for each verse 8
(1 mark off for each mistake. If more than 3 mistakes   —
in either verse, no marks for that verse)   **TOTAL 40**

50% — 20   70% — 28   80% — 32

STUDY NO. 2: GOD'S PLAN OF SALVATION
(Continued)

NOTES ON CORRECT ANSWERS

(The numbers in the lefthand margin correspond to the numbers of the correct answers on the previous page)

24-25. The Bible rules out every attempt of man to save himself, or to make himself righteous, apart from the grace of God received through faith in Christ.

25. The law was not given to make man righteous, but to show man that he is a sinner, and that he cannot save himself (See Rom. 3:20; 7:7-13).

26. Merely to "confess" sin, without "forsaking" it, does not procure for man the mercy of God (Compare Is. 55:7).

27. When God forgives sin, He also cleanses the sinner's heart. Thus cleansed, the sinner does not continue committing the sins which he has confessed.

28. Apart from the blood of Christ, man has no remedy for his own sinful heart.

29 (2). "Confess Jesus as Lord." This is more accurate than the King James translation. (Compare 1 Cor. 12:3 Phil. 2:11).

31. Note that the words of Jesus in Rev. 3:20 are addressed to a professing Christian Church (at Laodicea). But in spite of their profession, Christ Himself was left outside, seeking to gain admission. To how many Christian churches does this apply today? Christ's promise to "come in" is made to the individual, not to the congregation as a whole. The decision to receive Christ is always an individual matter.

32. "Power"— more correctly, "authority".

33. John 3:1-7 tells us that "we must be born again." John 1:12-13 tells us how we can be born again (of God). It is by receiving Christ as our personal Saviour and Lord.

34. In Rom. 6:23 notice the contrast; (a) "wages" = the due reward for the sins we have committed; (b) "gift" = the free, undeserved gift of God's grace.

38. The Christian life continues as it begins, "by faith". "As ye have received Christ Jesus the Lord, so walk ye in him" (Col. 2:6). We receive Christ by faith. We walk in Christ by faith (2 Cor. 5:7).

39. More literally: "I can do all things through Christ in me giving me the power" (Phil. 4:13).

40-41. Christ is "the high priest of our profession (confession)" (Heb. 3:1). His high-priestly ministry on our behalf is limited by the extent to which we "confess" Him. (Compare Heb. 4:14 and 10:21-23.) In the last resort, we have only 2 alternatives: to "confess", or to "deny".

44. "By the blood of the Lamb and the word of our testimony" means that we testify personally to what the Word of God says that the blood of Christ does for us. Here are some of the great benefits received through the blood of Christ: (1) redemption (Eph. 1:7); (2) cleansing (1 John 1:7); (3) justification (Rom. 5:9); (4) sanctification (Heb. 13:12).

45. Compare Rom. 12:21. In the last resort, there are only 2 alternatives: either to overcome, or to be overcome.

STUDY NO. 3

GOD'S PLAN FOR HEALING OUR BODIES

Introduction

By turning away from God in disobedience, man lost the blessing and protection of God, and came under a curse and the power of the devil. In this way, the devil was able to bring upon man's body many forms of pain and weakness and sickness. However, God in His mercy still desires to bless man, and to save him not only from sin, but also from sickness. For this reason Christ on the cross bore not only our sins, but also our sicknesses. Therefore, by faith in Christ we may now receive physical healing for our bodies, as well as forgiveness and peace for our souls.

Memory work: 1 Pet. 2:24   Please check when Memory card prepared ☐

(Review previous verses daily)

A. GENERAL:

WHO BRINGS SICKNESS AND WHO BRINGS HEALTH?

1. Who first deceived man, and tempted him to disobey God? (Gen. 3:1-13 1 John 3:8 Rev. 12:9)

   Serpent — devil or Satan

2. Why did pain, sickness and death first come to man? (Gen. 3:16-19)

   Because man disobeyed God

3. Who brought sickness upon Job? (Job 2:7)

   Satan — the devil

4. Who brought sickness on the woman here described, and how? (Luke 13:11, 16)

   ....

5. Who oppresses people with sickness? (Acts 10:38)

   ....

6. What does God promise to do for His people who obey Him? (Ex. 15:26)

   ....

   ....

7. What 2 things does God promise to do for His people who serve Him? (Ex. 23:25)

   (1)   ....

   (2)   ....

8. Do sicknesses belong to God's people or to their enemies? (Deut. 7:15)

   ....

9. What 2 things did David say the Lord did for him? (Psa. 103:3)

   (1)   ....

   (2)   ....

10. What 3 things did the apostle John wish for his Christian friend? (3 John 2)

    (1)   ....

    (2)   ....

    (3)   ....

11. How many of God's promises may we claim through faith in Christ? (2 Cor. 1:19, 20)

    ....

—14—

Stopped

12. For what purpose was Christ manifested to the world? (1 John 3:8)

....

13. For what purpose did God anoint Christ with the Holy Ghost? (Acts 10:38)

....

14. Whose will did Christ come to do? (John 5:30; 6:38)

....

15. Who worked Christ's miracles in Him? (John 10:37, 38; 14:10)

....

16. How many did Christ heal of those who came to Him? (Matt. 8:16; 12:15; 14: 35, 36 Luke 4:40; 6:19)

....

17. How many kinds of sickness did Christ heal? (Matt. 4:23, 24; 9:35)

....

18. When Christ did not heal many people, what was the reason? (Matt. 13:58, Mark 6:5, 6)

....

19. Does God ever change? (Mal. 3:6 Jam. 1:17) ....

20. Does Christ ever change? (Heb. 13:8) ....

B. THE PURPOSE OF CHRIST'S DEATH ON THE CROSS —

21. Mention 3 things which Christ bore in our place (Matt. 8:17 1 Pet. 2:24)

    (1) ....

    (2) ....

    (3) ....

22. As a result, what 3 consequences can we have in our lives? (1 Pet. 2:24)

    (1) ....

    (2) ....

    (3) ....

23. What was Christ made for us? (Gal. 3:13) ....

24. From what has Christ redeemed us? (Gal. 3:13)

....

25. How many kinds of sickness were included in the curse of the Law? (Deut. 28:15, 21, 22, 27, 28, 35, 59-61)

....

26. Which does God tell us to choose — blessing or curse? (Deut. 30:19)

....

Memory work: 1 Pet. 2:24

(This verse refers to Christ)

Write out this verse from memory.

....

....

....

....

DO NOT TURN THIS PAGE UNTIL YOU HAVE COMPLETED ALL ANSWERS IN THIS STUDY

STUDY NO. 3: GOD'S PLAN FOR HEALING OUR BODIES

CORRECT ANSWERS AND MARKS

Question No.	Answers	Marks
1.	The serpent — the devil — Satan	1
2.	Because man disobeyed God	1
3.	Satan — the devil	1
4.	Satan bound her with a spirit of infirmity	2
5.	The devil	1
6.	To put none of the diseases of Egypt upon them — to heal them	2
7.	(1) To bless their bread and water	1
	(2) To take sickness away from them	1
8.	To the enemies of God's people	1
9.	(1) The Lord forgave all his iniquities	1
	(2) The Lord healed all his diseases	1
10.	(1) That he might prosper	1
	(2) That he might be in health	1
	(3) That his soul might prosper	1
11.	All God's promises	1
12.	To destroy the works of the devil	1
13.	To do good and heal all that were oppressed of the devil	1
14.	The will of God the Father	1
15.	God the Father	1
16.	All — every one	1
17.	Every kind of sickness and disease	1
18.	The people's unbelief	1
19.	Never	1
20.	Never	1
21.	(1) Our infirmities (2) Our sicknesses (3) Our sins	3
22.	(1) We can be dead to sins	1
	(2) We can live unto righteousness	1
	(3) By His (Christ's) stripes we are healed	1
23.	A curse	1
24.	The curse of the law	1
25.	Every kind of sickness	1
26.	Blessing	1

Consult Bible for Written Memory Work

If word perfect, 4 marks	4
(1 mark off for each mistake. If	—
more than 3 mistakes, no marks)	TOTAL 40

50% — 20   70% — 28   80% — 32

STUDY NO. 3: GOD'S PLAN FOR HEALING OUR BODIES

NOTES ON CORRECT ANSWERS

(The numbers in the lefthand margin correspond to the numbers of the correct answers on the previous page)

1-2. Gen. ch. 3 reveals the root cause of all human sufferings, and traces it back to the devil. Jesus Himself said of the devil: "He was a murderer from the beginning" (John 8:44).

3-5. If we trace all sickness back to its source, the devil is the sole author of it. It is part of "the works of the devil".

6. An alternative translation: "I am Jehovah your Doctor" (Ex. 15:26).

9. Note the repetition of "all" with both "iniquities" and "diseases".

10. Note that Gaius, to whom John wrote, was a model believer, "walking in the truth" and "doing faithfully" his duty as a Christian (3 John 3-5).

11. 2 Cor. 1:20 rebuts dispensational theories which would rob Christians of the benefits of physical healing in this present dispensation. "ALL" God's promises are (NOW) for "US" (= all Christians). Applied personally: "Every promise that fits my situation and meets my need is for me now."

13. All 3 Persons of the Godhead are actively present in the ministry of healing. The FATHER anointed the SON with the SPIRIT. The result: healing for all.

14-15. Christ is the perfect manifestation of the Father's will. This applies to healing, as to all else that Christ did.

16-18. There is no record in the Gospels of any person who came to Christ for healing, who was not healed.

19-20. The unchanging truth of the gospel is based on the unchanging nature of God Himself.

21. Both Matthew and Peter are here quoting Is. 53:4-5. The correct literal translation of Is. 53:4 is: "Surely he has borne our sicknesses, and carried our pains." This refers to Christ. In 1 Pet. 2:24 the word translated "healed" is the basic Greek word for physical healing, from which the Greek word for "doctor" is derived.

24. "The curse of the law" means the curse that results from the breaking of the law. This curse is fully described in Deut. 28:15-68. It includes every form of sickness.

26. God sets forth 2 opposite pairs: either (a) "life" and "blessing"; or (b) "death" and "cursing". It is left to man to choose.

STUDY NO. 4

GOD'S PLAN FOR HEALING OUR BODIES

(Continued)

Introduction

Healing for our bodies from God comes to us through hearing and believing God's Word, and through allowing God's Spirit to fill our bodies with the resurrection life of Christ. Not only may we receive healing for our own bodies in this way, but we may also offer healing and deliverance to others in the name of Jesus. Two main ways in which we may do this are by laying our hands on the sick and praying for them, or by getting believing church elders to anoint them with oil in the name of the Lord. If we act in faith in this way, God will work with us and confirm the truth of His Word by miracles of healing and deliverance.

Memory work: Mark 16:17, 18

Please check when Memory card prepared ☐

(Review previous verse daily)

C. 3 MEANS OF HEALING:

(1) God's Word, (2) God's Spirit, (3) Our Faith.

27. What does God send to heal and deliver us? (Psa. 107:20)

....

28. Mention two things which God's words bring to His children (Prov. 4:20-22)

(1) ....

(2) ....

29. If God's Spirit dwells in us, what will it do for our mortal bodies? (Rom. 8:11)

....

30. What does God want to manifest in our mortal bodies? (2 Cor. 4:10, 11)

....

31. What did Jesus look for in those who came to Him for healing? (Matt. 9:28, 29 Mark 2:5; 9:23 Luke 8:50)

....

32. How did Peter explain the healing of a lame man? (Acts 3:16)

....

....

33. What did Paul perceive in the cripple at Lystra which enabled him to be healed? (Acts 14:8-10)

....

34. How does faith come to us? (Rom. 10:17)

....

D. THE AUTHORITY COMMITTED TO BELIEVERS

35. Mention 2 kinds of power which Christ gave to His disciples (Matt. 10:1)

(1) ....

(2) ....

36. Mention 4 things which Christ commanded His disciples to do. (Matt. 10:8)

(1) ....

(2) ....

(3) ....

(4) ....

37. When the disciples failed to heal an epileptic, what 2 reasons did Jesus give? (Matt. 17:20, 21 Mark 9:29)

(1) ....

(2) ....

38. What two things did Jesus say that a person who believed in Him would be able to do? (John 14:12)

(1) ....

(2) ....

39. What may believers do for sick people in the name of Jesus? (Mark 16:17, 18)

....

....

40. What will happen to such sick people? (Mark 16:18)

....

41. What should a sick Christian do? (Jam. 5:14)

....

42. What 2 things should church elders do for a sick Christian? (Jam. 5:14)

(1) ....

(2) ....

43. What 2 things will the Lord for such a Christian? (Jam. 5:15)

(1) ....

(2) ....

44. What kind of prayer will save the sick? (Jam. 5:15)

....

45. What 2 things did the disciples pray that God would do in the name of Jesus? (Acts 4:30)

(1) ....

(2) ....

46. When the disciples went out and preached, what 2 things did the Lord do for them? (Mark 16:20)

(1) ....

(2) ....

Memory work: Mark 16:17, 18

Write out these verses from memory.

....

....

....

....

....

....

DO NOT TURN THIS PAGE UNTIL YOU HAVE COMPLETED ALL ANSWERS IN THIS STUDY

STUDY NO. 4: GOD'S PLAN FOR HEALING OUR BODIES
(Continued)

CORRECT ANSWERS AND MARKS

Question No.	Answers	Marks
27.	His (God's) Word	1
28.	(1) Life (2) Health to all their flesh	2
29.	It will quicken (= give life to) our mortal bodies	1
30.	The life of Jesus	1
31.	Faith	1
32.	Faith in the name of Jesus had healed him	2
33.	The cripple had faith to be healed	1
34.	By hearing the word of God	2
35.	(1) Power against unclean spirits to cast them out	2
	(2) Power to heal all manner of sickness and disease	2
36.	(1) To heal the sick (2) To cleanse the lepers	2
	(3) To raise the dead (4) To cast out devils	2
37.	(1) Because of their unbelief	1
	(2) It could only come out through prayer and fasting	1
38.	(1) The works that He did (2) Greater works than these	2
39.	Believers may lay hands on the sick in the name of Jesus	1
40.	They will recover	1
41.	He should call for the elders of the church	1
42.	(1) Pray over him	1
	(2) Anoint him with oil in the name of the Lord (= Jesus)	1
43.	(1) Raise him up	1
	(2) Forgive him if he has committed sins	1
44.	The prayer of faith	1
45.	(1) Stretch forth His hand to heal	1
	(2) Grant signs and wonders to be done	1
46.	(1) The Lord worked with them	1
	(2) He confirmed the word with signs following	2

Consult Bible for Written Memory Work

If word perfect, 4 marks for each verse 8
(1 mark off for each mistake. If more than 3 —
mistakes in either verse, no marks for that verse)   TOTAL 44

50% — 22   70% — 31   80% — 35

STUDY NO. 4: GOD'S PLAN FOR HEALING OUR BODIES
(Continued)

NOTES ON CORRECT ANSWERS

(The numbers in the lefthand margin correspond to the numbers of the correct answers on the previous page)

27-34. Psa. 33:6 describes the means used by God in creation: "By the WORD of the Lord ... and by the BREATH (= SPIRIT) of his mouth." All creation is by the WORD and the SPIRIT of God, working together. The same is true of God's re-creative work of healing. This is done by his WORD and His SPIRIT working together. The means by which we receive this work of healing is our FAITH.

28. Prov. 4:20-22. The alternative translation of 'health" is " medicine". These verses are God's great "medicine bottle". However, this medicine must be taken according to the directions, which are fourfold: (1) "Attend ..." (2) "Incline thine ear" (be humble and teachable) (3) "Let them not not depart from thine eyes" (4) "Keep them in the midst of thine heart." The 4 channels to receive the medicine are the mind, the ear, the eye, and the heart.

30. 2 Cor. 4:10-11. God's will is that the resurrection life of Christ should be "manifested" (= openly revealed) in our "mortal flesh". This is God's provision of healing, health and vitality for our bodies in this present life.

34. Rom. 10:17. First, God's Word produces "hearing". Then out of "hearing" there develops " faith". The process of "hearing" is described in its 4 phases in Prov. 4:20-21.

35-36. In the New Testament, no one is ever sent out to preach without also being commissioned to heal and to deliver from evil spirits. With Matt. 10:8 compare Matt. 28:20. "Teaching them to observe all things whatsoever I have commanded you: and, lo, I am with you always, even unto the end of the world" (= this present age). Christ made provision that exactly the same ministry which He instituted with the first 12 disciples should be continued unchanged by each succeeding generation of disciples until the end of the present age.

37 (2). Jesus Himself practised fasting, and He expected His disciples to follow Him in this also (Matt. 6:16-18). However, the disciples did not do this as long as Jesus ("the bridegroom") remained with them on earth (Mark 2:18-20).

38. The ministry of Jesus is the pattern for all Christian ministry. The Holy Spirit, sent by Jesus after He had returned to the Father, performs these works, promised by Jesus, through His believing disciples.

39. The promises of Mark 16:17-18 apply generally to "them that believe"—to all believers.

39-44. For further teaching on this subject, see my book "Laying On Of Hands".

41. A sick Christian who does not call for the elders of the church is disobedient.

45. Acts 4:30 is still a pattern prayer for the Christian church.

STUDY NO. 5

THE BIBLE: THE WORD OF GOD

Introduction

The Bible is God's own Word, His great gift to all men everywhere, to help them out of their sin and misery and darkness. The Bible is not an ordinary book, but the men who wrote it were inspired and moved by God's Holy Spirit to write exactly the truth as God gave it to them. Every word is true, filled with God's own power and authority. We should read our Bible as if it was God Himself speaking to us directly and personally. It will impart to us light, understanding, spiritual food and physical health. It will cleanse us, sanctify us, build us up, make us partakers of God's own nature. It will give us power and wisdom to overcome the devil.

Memory work: 2 Tim. 3:16, 17 → Due July 15th in S.S.

Please check when Memory card prepared ☐

(Review previous verses daily)

Q's 1-11 July 8th

1. What name did Jesus give to the scripture? (John 10:35)

....

2. What did Jesus say about the scripture which shows its authority? (John 10:35)

....

3. Write down 2 things which David tells us about God's Word.
   (1) (Psa. 119:89) ....
   (2) (Psa. 119:160) ....

4. How were the scriptures originally given?
   (1) (2 Tim. 3:16) ....
   (2) (2 Pet. 1:20-21) ....

5. What kind of seed must a person receive into his heart, in order to be born again and have eternal life? (1 Pet. 1:23)

....

6. Write down 4 things for which the scriptures are profitable to a Christian (2 Tim. 3:16)
   (1) .... (2) ....
   (3) .... (4) ....

7. What is the final result in a Christian who studies and obeys God's Word? (2 Tim. 3:17)

....

....

8. What is the spiritual food which God has provided for His children? (1 Pet. 2:2 Matt. 4:4)

....

9. How much did Job esteem God's Words? (Job. 23:12)

....

10. When Jeremiah fed on God's Word, what did it become to him? (Jer. 15:16)

....

11. How can a young Christian person lead a clean life? (Psa. 119:9)

....

12. Why should a Christian hide (store up) God's Word in his heart? (Psa. 119:11)

....

13. What 2 results does God's Word produce in young men, when it abides in them? (1 John 2:14)

(1) ....

(2) ....

14. How did Jesus answer the devil each time He was tempted? (Matt. 4:4, 7, 10)

....

15. What is the sword which God has given to Christians as part of their spiritual armour? (Eph. 6:17)

....

16. In what 2 ways does God's Word show Christians how to walk in this world? (Psa. 119:105)

(1) ....

(2) ....

17. What 2 things does God's word give to the mind of a Christian? (Psa. 119:130)

(1) ....   (2) ....

18. What does God's Word provide for the body of a Christian who studies it carefully? (Prov. 4:20-22)

....

19. When God's people were sick and in need, what did God send to heal and deliver them? (Psa. 107:20)

....

20. Write down 4 things, mentioned in the following verses, which God's Word does for His people:

(1) (John 15:3 Eph. 5:26) ....

(2) (John 17:17) ....

(3) (Acts 20:32) ....

(4) (Acts 20:32) ....

21. How does a Christian prove his love for Christ? (John 14:21)

....

22. Whom did Jesus call His mother and His brethren? (Luke 8:21)

....

23. How is God's love made perfect in a Christian? (1 John 2:5)

....

24. Write down 2 results which follow in our lives when we claim the promises of God's Word (2 Pet. 1:4)

(1) ....

(2) ....

Memory work: 2 Tim. 3:16, 17 → Due Aug. 12th in S.S.

Write out these verses from memory.

....

....

....

....

....

....

DO NOT TURN THIS PAGE UNTIL YOU HAVE COMPLETED ALL ANSWERS IN THIS STUDY

Q's 12-12 Aug. 5th

STUDY NO. 5: THE BIBLE: THE WORD OF GOD

CORRECT ANSWERS AND MARKS

Question No.	Answers	Marks
1.	The Word of God	1
2.	It cannot be broken	1
3.	(1) It is settled forever in heaven	1
	(2) It is true from the beginning	1
4.	(1) By inspiration of God	1
	(2) Holy men of God spoke as they were moved by the Holy Ghost	2
5.	The incorruptible seed of God's Word	2
6.	(1) Doctrine (2) Reproof (3) Correction	3
	(4) Instruction in righteousness	1
7.	He is made perfect (= complete)—thoroughly furnished (= equipped) for all good works	2
8.	The Word of God	1
9.	More than his necessary food	1
10.	The joy and rejoicing of his heart	1
11.	By taking heed to it according to God's Word	2
12.	That he may not sin against God	1
13.	(1) It makes them strong	1
	(2) They overcome the wicked one (= the devil)	1
14.	He answered from the written Word of God	1
15.	The Word of God	1
16.	(1) It is a light to their path	1
	(2) It is a lamp to their feet	1
17.	(1) Light (2) Understanding	2
18.	Health to all his flesh	1
19.	His (God's) Word	1
20.	(1) It cleanses — washes, like clean water	1
	(2) It sanctifies (3) It edifies	2
	(4) It gives them their inheritance	1
21.	He has Christ's commandments and keeps them	2
22.	Those who hear the Word of God and do it	1
23.	By keeping God's Word	1
24.	(1) We are made partakers of the divine nature	1
	(2) We escape the corruption of this world	1

Consult Bible for Written Memory Work

If word perfect, 4 marks for each verse 8
(1 mark off for each mistake. If more than —
3 mistakes in either verse, no marks for that verse)   TOTAL 49

50% — 24   70% — 34   80% — 39

STUDY NO. 5: THE BIBLE: THE WORD OF GOD

NOTES ON CORRECT ANSWERS

(The numbers in the lefthand margin correspond to the numbers of the correct answers on the previous page)

1-2. It is perfectly clear that Jesus accepted the Old Testament scriptures, without question or reservation, as the inspired, authoritative Word of God. He based all His teaching on these scriptures, and directed the whole course of His own life to obey and fulfil them.

3. God's Word originates in heaven. Men were the channels through whom this Word was given, but God Himself is the source of it.

4(1). "By inspiration of God" = literally "God-inbreathed". The words "breath" and "spirit" are the same in both Hebrew and Greek. (For a full study of the inspiration and authority of the Bible, see my book, "Foundation For Faith".)

5. The "incorruptible seed" of God's Word, received by faith in the heart, and caused to germinate there by the Holy Spirit, brings forth divine, eternal, incorruptible life.

6-8. Note: "ALL scripture" (2 Tim. 3:16), "EVERY word" (Matt. 4:4). For full spiritual development, a Christian must study and apply the teachings of the whole Bible.

8-10. God's Word provides food suited to every stage of spiritual development: (1) "Milk" for new born babes (1 Pet. 2:2) (2) "Bread" for those growing up (Matt. 4:4) (3) "Strong meat" (full diet) for those who are "of full age" (spiritually mature) (Heb. 5:12-14).

11. "By taking heed thereto," etc.: i.e. by carefully applying the teaching of God's Word to every phase of his life.

12. Someone has said: "Either God's Word will keep you from sin, or sin will keep you from God's Word."

13-15. In Eph. 6:13-17 Paul lists 6 items of spiritual armour which provide the Christian with complete protection, but of them all there is only one weapon of attack, "the sword of the Spirit". It is the responsibility of each believer to "take" this sword.

16. Compare 1 John 1:7, "If we walk in the light ..." The "light" by which we must walk is God's Word.

17-19. God's Word provides for the spirit, the mind and the body of the Christian.

20(4). Only through God's Word do we come to know what is our rightful inheritance in Christ, and how to obtain that inheritance.

21-23. "The keeping of God's Word is the supreme distinguishing feature which should mark you out from the world as a disciple of Christ ...

"Your attitude toward God's Word is your attitude toward God Himself. You do not love God more than you love His Word. You do not obey God more than you obey His Word. You do not honour God more than you honour His Word. You do not have more room in your heart and life for God than you have for His Word." ("Foundation For Faith" page 20.)

24. Through God's Word, believed and obeyed, God's own nature permeates the heart and life of the Christian, replacing the old corrupt Adamic nature.

STUDY NO. 6

THE HOLY SPIRIT

Introduction

In all His earthly ministry Jesus was completely dependent upon the Holy Spirit. Before the Holy Spirit descended upon Him at the river Jordan, He never preached a sermon or performed a miracle. After that, all He did was by the power of the Holy Spirit. When He was about to leave His disciples, He promised that from heaven He would send the Holy Spirit to them in their turn, to be their Comforter and to supply all their spiritual needs. This promise was fulfilled on the day of Pentecost when they were all baptised in the Holy Spirit. NOTE: The two English expressions "Holy Spirit" and "Holy Ghost" are two different ways of translating one and the same expression in the original Greek of the New Testament. There is therefore no difference in meaning between these two expressions.

Due Aug. 19th in S. S.

Memory work: Acts 2:38, 39 Please check when Memory card prepared ☐

(Review previous verses daily)

Q's 1-10 Aug. 12th

1. With what did God the Father anoint Jesus for His earthly ministry? (Acts 10:38)

   ....

2. What did John the Baptist see descend and abide upon Jesus? (John 1:32-33)

   ....

3. What did Jesus say was upon Him, enabling Him to preach and to minister to those in need? (Luke 4:18)

   ....

4. By what power did Jesus say He cast out devils? (Matt. 12:28)

   ....

5. Whom did Jesus say He would send to His disciples from the Father after He Himself returned to heaven? (John 14:16, 26; 15:26)

   ....

6. What two expressions does Jesus use to describe the Comforter?

   (1) (John 14:17) ....

   (2) (John 14:26) ....

7. Write down 2 things which Jesus says the Holy Spirit will do for the disciples (John 14:26)

   (1) ....

   (2) ....

8. Write down another way in which Jesus says the Holy Spirit will help the disciples (John 16:13)

   ....

9. Write down 2 ways in which the Holy Spirit will reveal Jesus to His disciples.

   (1) (John 15:26) ....

   (2) (John 16:14) ....

Aug. 12ᵗʰ 10. After what did Jesus say that the disciples would receive power to become effective witnesses for Him? (Acts 1:8)

....

11. What did John the Baptist tell the people that Jesus would do for them? (Mark 1:8)

....

12. What promise did Jesus give to His disciples just before He ascended into heaven? (Acts 1:5)

....

13. What did Jesus tell His disciples to do until this promise should be fulfilled? (Luke 24:49)

....

....

14. Upon what day was this promise to these disciples fulfilled? (Acts 2:1-4)

....

15. Why could the Holy Spirit not be given to the disciples during the earthly ministry of Jesus? (John 7:39)

....

16. After Jesus had returned to His position of glory at the right hand of God, what did He receive from the Father? (Acts 2:33)

....

?'s 11-21
Sept. 2nd

17. How could the unbelievers present know that Jesus had poured out the Holy Spirit upon His disciples? (Acts 2:33)

....

18. What could these unbelievers hear the disciples doing through the power of the Holy Spirit? (Acts 2:7-8)

....

19. Upon whom does God promise to pour out His Spirit at the close of this age? (Acts 2:17)

....

20. To whom does Peter say that the promised gift of the Holy Spirit is made available? (Acts 2:39)

....

....

21. What good gift will God the Father give to all His children who ask Him for it? (Luke 11:13)

....

Memory work: Acts 2:38, 39 → *Due Sept. 9ᵗʰ*

Write out these verses from memory

....
....
....
....
....
....

DO NOT TURN THIS PAGE UNTIL YOU HAVE COMPLETED ALL ANSWERS IN THIS STUDY

STUDY NO. 6: THE HOLY SPIRIT

CORRECT ANSWERS AND MARKS

Question No.	Answers	Marks
1.	With the Holy Ghost and power	1
2.	The (Holy) Spirit	1
3.	The Spirit of the Lord	1
4.	By the Spirit of God	1
5.	The Comforter	1
6.	(1) The Spirit of truth	1
	(2) The Holy Ghost	1
7.	(1) Teach you all things	1
	(2) Bring all things to your remembrance whatsoever I have said unto you	2
8.	He will guide you into all the truth	1
9.	(1) He shall testify of me (Jesus)	1
	(2) He shall glorify me (Jesus)	1
10.	After that the Holy Ghost is come upon you	1
11.	He shall baptise you with the Holy Ghost	1
12.	Ye shall be baptised with the Holy Ghost not many days hence	2
13.	Tarry ye in the city of Jerusalem, until ye be endued with power from on high	2
14.	The day of Pentecost	1
15.	Because Jesus was not yet glorified	1
16.	The promise of the Holy Ghost	1
17.	They could see and hear it	1
18.	Speaking in the tongues (languages) of the countries in which the unbelievers had been born	2
19.	Upon all flesh	1
20.	To you, and to your children, and to all that are afar off, even as many as the Lord our God shall call	3
21.	The Holy Spirit	1

Consult Bible for Written Memory Work

If word perfect, 4 marks for each verse		8
(1 mark off for each mistake. If more than		—
3 mistakes in either verse, no marks for that verse)	TOTAL	38

50% — 19   70% — 27   80% — 30

STUDY NO. 6: THE HOLY SPIRIT

NOTES ON CORRECT ANSWERS

(The numbers in the lefthand margin correspond to the numbers of the correct answers on the previous page)

1-5. The English word "Christ" is taken from a Greek word which means "Anointed." It thus corresponds exactly to the Hebrew title, "Messiah", which also means "Anointed". In historical experience Jesus became the "Messiah", the "Anointed One", when the Holy Spirit descended and abode upon Him, after His baptism by John the Baptist. The title "Christ", or "Messiah", indicates that the whole earthly ministry of Jesus was made possible by the "anointing" of the Holy Spirit. It is God's purpose that the same "anointing" of the Holy Spirit should be the abiding portion of all Christians. "Now he which establisheth us with you in Christ, and hath anointed us, is God" (2 Cor. 1:21). "But the anointing which ye have received of him abideth in you ..." (1 John 2:27). 'Christians" are literally "anointed ones". For effective Christian living, the disciple is as much dependent upon the Holy Spirit, as Jesus Himself was.

5-6. "Comforter" = "Advocate" — "One called in alongside". The same word is used of Jesus in 1 John 2:1. Christ pleads the cause of the believer in heaven. The Holy Spirit, through the believer, pleads the cause of Christ on earth (see Matt. 10:19-20).

6-9. In John 16:7 Jesus said: "It is expedient for you that I go away: for if I go not away, the Comforter will not come unto you; but if I depart, I will send him unto you." When Jesus returned to heaven and sent the Holy Spirit upon the disciples, they immediately received a better knowledge and understanding of Jesus Himself, than they had had all the time that He was actually present with them on earth. Thus the Holy Spirit fulfilled His ministry to reveal, interpret and glorify the person, the work and the message of Christ.

11. John the Baptist's introduction of Jesus as "the baptiser in the Holy Spirit" is placed at the forefront of all 4 Gospels. The New Testament places the greatest possible emphasis upon this aspect of Christ's ministry. The Christian church should do the same.

12-13. The Gospels close, as they open, with the promise of the baptism in the Holy Spirit.

15-16. By His death on the cross, Jesus purchased for every believer the gift of the Holy Spirit (See Gal. 3:13-14). After His resurrection and ascension, it was His unique privilege to receive this gift from the Father and to bestow it upon His disciples.

17-18. All through the New Testament the baptism in the Holy Spirit is attested by the supernatural evidence of speaking with other tongues.

18-21. At the close of this age God has promised a final, worldwide outpouring of the Holy Spirit. Every Christian has the scriptural right to ask God for this gift.

STUDY NO. 7

RESULTS OF THE BAPTISM IN THE HOLY SPIRIT

Introduction

The baptism in the Holy Spirit is a supernatural enduement with power from heaven to equip the Christian for effective witness and service. It is attested by speaking in a language given by the Holy Spirit, but unkown to the one speaking. It enables the Christian to build up his own spiritual life by direct and continual communion with God, and is the gateway into a life in which both the gifts and the fruits of the Holy Spirit should be manifested. In the New Testament church, this experience was considered normal for all believers.

Due Sept. 16th in S.S.

Memory work: Acts 2:17,18 Please check when Memory card prepared ☐

(Review previous verses daily)

*Q's
1 -12
Sept. 9th*

1. What happened to the disciples on the day of Pentecost when they were all filled with the Holy Ghost? (Acts 2:4)

....

....

2. Through whose preaching did the people in Samaria come to believe in Jesus Christ? (Acts 8:12)

....

3. When Peter and John came down to Samaria, how did they pray for the Christians there? (Acts 8:15)

....

4. How did the Christians at Samaria receive the Holy Ghost? (Acts 8:17)

....

5. How did Saul of Tarsus (Paul) receive the Holy Ghost? (Acts 9:17)

....

6. As Peter was preaching to the people in the house of Cornelius, what happened to all who heard him? (Acts 10:44)

....

7. How did Peter and his companions know that all these people in the house of Cornelius had received the Holy Ghost? (Acts 10:45-46)

....

8. What question did Paul ask the disciples at Ephesus? (Acts 19:2)

....

9. How did these disciples at Ephesus receive the Holy Ghost? (Acts 19:6)

....

10. What happened after the Holy Ghost came on these disciples? (Acts 19:6)

....

11. How much did Paul say that he himself spoke in tongues? (1 Cor. 14:18)

....

12. Write down 3 things that a Christian does when he speaks in an unknown tongue? (1 Cor. 14:2, 4)

(1) ....

(2) ....

(3) ....

—30—

13. If a Christian prays in an unknown tongue, what part of him is then praying? (1 Cor. 14:14)

....

14. How did Jesus say that true worshippers should worship God? (John 4:23-24)

....

15. How does Jude exhort Christians to build themselves up in their faith? (Jude 20)

....

16. When a Christian speaks in an unknown tongue, what may he pray for next? (1 Cor. 14:13)

....

17. In a public meeting where there is no interpreter, how may a Christian speak in an unknown tongue? (1 Cor. 14:28)

....

18. Did Paul say that he wished that all Christians spoke in tongues? (1 Cor. 14:5)

....

19. How many Christians did Paul say may prophesy? (1 Cor. 14:31)

....

20. Should Christians be ignorant about spiritual gifts? (1 Cor. 12:1)

....

Q's 13-26
Oct. 7th

21. Make a list of the 9 gifts of the Spirit (1 Cor. 12:8-10)
    (1) .... (2) ....
    (3) .... (4) ....
    (5) .... (6) ....
    (7) .... (8) ....
    (9) ....

22. Make a list of the 9 fruits of the Spirit (Gal. 5:22-23)
    (1) .... (2) .... (3) ....
    (4) .... (5) .... (6) ....
    (7) .... (8) .... (9) ....

23. Should a Christian have spiritual gifts without spiritual fruit? (1 Cor. 13:1-2)

....

24. Should a Christian have spiritual fruit without spiritual gifts? (1 Cor. 12:31; 14:1)

....

25. Write down 3 supernatural occurences that will result from the outpouring of the Holy Spirit at the end of this age (Acts 2:17)
    (1) ....
    (2) ....
    (3) ....

26. Write down 5 different spiritual contributions that a Christian may make at a meeting with fellow Christians (1 Cor. 14:26)
    (1) .... (2) .... (3) ....
    (4) .... (5) ....

Memory work: Acts 2:17, 18 → *Due Oct. 14th in S.S.*

Write out these verses from memory

....
....
....
....
....

DO NOT TURN THIS PAGE UNTIL YOU HAVE COMPLETED ALL ANSWERS IN THIS STUDY

STUDY NO. 7: RESULTS OF THE BAPTISM IN THE HOLY SPIRIT

CORRECT ANSWERS AND MARKS

Question No.	Answers	Marks
1.	They spoke with other tongues as the Spirit gave them utterance	2
2.	The preaching of Philip	1
3.	That they might receive the Holy Ghost	1
4.	They (i.e. Peter and John) laid their hands on them	1
5.	Ananias put his hands upon him	1
6.	The Holy Ghost fell on them all	1
7.	They heard them speak with tongues and magnify God	1
8.	Have ye received the Holy Ghost since ye believed?	1
9.	Paul laid his hands upon them	1
10.	They spoke with tongues and prophesied	1
11.	More than ye all (i.e. more than all the Christians at Corinth)	1
12.	(1) He speaks to God (not to men)	1
	(2) He speaks mysteries	1
	(3) He edifies himself	1
13.	His spirit	1
14.	In spirit and in truth	1
15.	By praying always in the Holy Ghost	1
16.	That he may interpret	1
17.	He may speak to himself and to God	1
18.	Yes	1
19.	All	1
20.	No	1
21.	(1) The word of wisdom (2) The word of knowledge	2
	(3) Faith (4) Gifts of healing	2
	(5) Working of miracles (6) Prophecy	2
	(7) Discerning of spirits (8) Divers kinds of tongues	2
	(9) Interpretation of tongues	1
22.	(1) Love (2) Joy (3) Peace	3
	(4) Longsuffering (5) Gentleness (6) Goodness	3
	(7) Faith (8) Meekness (9) Temperance	3
23.	No	1
24.	No	1
25.	(1) Your sons and your daughters shall prophesy	1
	(2) Your young men shall see visions	1
	(3) Your old men shall dream dreams	1
26.	(1) A psalm (2) A doctrine (3) A tongue	3
	(4) A revelation (5) An interpretation	2

Consult Bible for Written Memory Work

If word perfect, 4 marks for each verse 8

(1 mark off for each mistake. If more than 3 .... —

mistakes in either verse, no marks for that verse)   TOTAL 59

50% — 29   70% — 41   80% — 47

STUDY NO. 7: RESULTS OF THE BAPTISM IN THE HOLY SPIRIT

NOTES ON CORRECT ANSWERS

(The numbers in the lefthand margin correspond to the numbers of the correct answers on the previous page)

1. "Out of the abundance of the heart the mouth speaketh" (Matt. 12:34). The first outflow of the Holy Spirit is from the believer's mouth.

2-4. Through the ministry of Philip, multitudes in Samaria had been wonderfully saved and healed. But this was not sufficient for the apostles. They expected all new converts to receive the baptism in the Holy Spirit. This came to these converts in Samaria through the ministry of Peter and John, as a separate experience, subsequent to salvation.

5. Laying on of hands to impart the Holy Spirit was not confined to apostles. Ananias is merely called a "disciple" (Acts 9:10). Nor is laying on of hands always needed to impart the Holy Spirit. In Acts 2:2-4 and 10:44-46 the believers received without any laying on of hands.

8-10. At Ephesus, as at Samaria, these disciples received the baptism in the Holy Spirit as a separate experience, subsequent to salvation. As in Acts 2:4 and 10:46, their experience culminated in speaking with other tongues (and also, in this case, prophesying).

11-15. After receiving the baptism in the Holy Spirit, the primary use of speaking in another tongue is for personal worship and prayer. The believer does not understand with his mind what he is saying, but his spirit holds direct communion with God, and in this way he is able to edify (build up) himself.

16-17. Through the gift of interpretation Christians may come to know the meaning of an utterance previously given in an unknown tongue. In public meetings an utterance given out loud in an unknown tongue should normally be followed by the interpretation. If there is no one to interpret, the believer may speak in an unknown tongue "to himself and to God."

19. To "prophesy" is to speak by the supernatural inspiration of the Holy Spirit in a language understood by the speaker and by those spoken to.

21-24. There is an important logical distinction between "gifts" and "fruit". A "gift" is imparted and received by a momentary act. "Fruit" is cultivated by time and labour (See 2 Tim. 2:6). Consider the difference between a Christmas tree with its gifts, and an apple tree with its fruit. Spiritually, gifts are not a substitute for fruit, and fruit is not a substitute for gifts. God's provision is for all Christians to have both. (Note that "love" is never called a "gift".)

25-26. The full outpouring of the Holy Spirit always produces a variety of supernatural manifestations. Through these, Christians are able to minister to one another on a level higher than that of natural ability or education.

STUDY NO. 8

WORSHIP AND PRAYER

Introduction

Prayer is the great means by which Christians come into the presence of God, to worship Him, and to receive from Him the guidance, the help, and the strength which they need at all times. Every Christian should set aside regular times each day, to spend in personal prayer and Bible reading. The most powerful and influential person in the world is the Christian who knows how to pray and to get his prayers answered. To be able to pray in this way we must follow carefully the instructions of God's Word, which are set out in this study, and we must have the help of the Holy Spirit.

Due Oct. 21st in S.S.

Memory work: John 15:7   Please check when Memory card prepared ☐

(Review previous verses daily)

1. What kind of people is God seeking? (John 4:23, 24)

   ....

2. In whose prayer does the Lord delight? (Prov. 15:8)

   ....

3. What kind of prayer produces great results? (Jam. 5:16)

   ....

4. If we wish God to hear our prayers, what 2 things must we do? (John 9:31)
   (1) .... (2) ....

5. By what may we enter boldly into the holy presence of God? (Heb. 10:19)

   ....

6. With what 2 things should we enter God's presence? (Psa. 100:4)
   (1) .... (2) ....

7. What should a Christian do instead of worrying? (Phil. 4:6)

   ....

   ....

8. In whose name should we pray, and with what motive? (John 14:13)

   ....

9. Upon what 2 conditions may we ask for what we will from God? (John 15:7)
   (1) ....
   (2) ....

10. Write down 4 things, found in the following verses, which will hinder the answers to our prayers:
    (1) (Psa. 66:18) ....
    (2) (Jam. 1:6, 7) ....
    (3) (Jam. 4:3) ....
    (4) (1 Pet. 3:7) ....

11. In order to overcome Satanic forces, what must we sometimes join with prayer? (Mark 9:29)

    ....

12. In order to receive the things that we desire, what must we do when we pray? (Mark 11:24)

    ....

Q's 1- 12 Oct. 14th

—34—

13. If we have anything against other people when we pray, what must we do first? (Mark 11:25)

....

14. If we forgive others when we pray, how will God deal with us? (Mark 11:25)

....

15. If we do not forgive others, how will God deal with us? (Mark 11:26)

....

16. If we pray according to the will of God, of what 2 things may we be confident? (1 John 5:14, 15)

   (1) ....

   (2) ....

17. How did David say he would begin each day? (Psa. 5:3)

....

18. At what 3 times did David decide to pray each day? (Psa. 55:17)

   (1) .... (2) .... (3) ....

19. Apart from such regular times of prayer, how often should we pray? (Eph. 6:18 1 Thes. 5:17)

....

20. When we do not have strength or knowledge to pray aright, who helps us to pray according to God's will? (Rom. 8:26, 27)

....

21. If we are praying alone, what does Jesus tell us to do? (Matt. 6:6)

....

22. How does Jesus say that this kind of prayer will be rewarded? (Matt. 6:6)

....

23. If we meet with other Christians for prayer in the name of Jesus, what promise has Jesus given us? (Matt. 18:20)

....

24. What should be our attitude toward other Christians with whom we pray? (Matt. 18:19)

....

25. For whom should we pray especially? (1 Tim. 2:1, 2)

....

26. What position of the body does Paul here recommend for prayer? (1 Tim 2:8)

....

27. What 2 wrong mental attitudes must we guard against when praying? (1 Tim. 2:8)

   (1) .... (2) ....

28. What is the result of getting our prayers answered (John 16:24)

....

Memory work: John 15:7

Write out this verse from memory.

....

....

....

....

DO NOT TURN THIS PAGE UNTIL YOU HAVE COMPLETED ALL ANSWERS IN THIS STUDY

STUDY NO. 8: WORSHIP AND PRAYER

CORRECT ANSWERS AND MARKS

Question No.	Answers	Marks
1.	True worshippers, who will worship God in spirit and in truth	2
2.	The prayer of the upright	1
3.	The effectual fervent prayer of a righteous man	2
4.	(1) Worship God (2) Do God's will	2
5.	By the blood of Jesus	1
6.	(1) Thanksgiving (2) Praise	2
7.	In everything by prayer and supplication with thanksgiving make known his requests to God	3
8.	In the name of Jesus, for God to be glorified	2
9.	(1) If we abide in Christ	1
	(2) If His words abide in us	1
10.	(1) If we "regard iniquity" (tolerate known sin) in our heart	1
	(2) If we waver and do not ask in faith	1
	(3) If we ask amiss, to gratify our own lusts	1
	(4) A wrong relationship between husband and wife	1
11.	Fasting	1
12.	Believe that we receive them (at the time of praying)	1
13.	We must forgive them	1
14.	God will forgive us	1
15.	God will not forgive us	1
16.	(1) That God hears us	1
	(2) That we have the petitions that we desired	1
17.	By directing his prayer to God and looking up	2
18.	(1) Evening (2) Morning (3) Noon	3
18.	Always, without ceasing	1
20.	The Holy Spirit	1
21.	Enter into our closet and shut the door	1
22.	Our heavenly Father will reward us openly	1
23.	Jesus Himself is in the midst	1
24.	We should agree with them concerning anything that we ask	2
25.	For kings and all in authority	1
26.	Lifting up holy hands	1
27.	(1) Wrath (2) Doubting	2
28.	Our joy is full	1

Consult Bible for Written Memory Work

If word perfect, 4 marks 4
(1 mark off for each mistaks. If   —
more than 3 mistakes, no marks)   TOTAL 49

50% — 24   70% — 34   80% — 39

STUDY NO. 8: WORSHIP AND PRAYER

NOTES ON CORRECT ANSWERS

(The numbers in the lefthand margin correspond to the numbers of the correct answers on the previous page)

The whole Bible — and especially the New Testament — emphasises both the willingness and the ability of God to answer prayer (See Matt. 7:7-8). Indeed, God is more willing to answer prayer, than men are to pray. However, in order to receive the answers to our prayers, we must meet the conditions stated in God's Word. Most of the answers in this study deal with these conditions, which may be summarised as follows:

5, 8, 23. ACCESS ONLY THROUGH CHRIST. As sinners, we can be reconciled to God only through the propitiatory sacrifice and the mediatorial ministry of Christ. In recognition of this, we come to God through the name and the blood of Jesus.

1, 4(1), 6, 7. RIGHT APPROACH: worship, thanksgiving, praise.

1, 2, 3, 4(2), 9(1). RIGHT CHARACTER: truth, uprightness, righteousness, obeddience (all possible only as we "abide in Christ").

8, 10(3). RIGHT MOTIVE: for God's glory, not to gratify our own lusts.

10(4), 13, 14, 15, 24, 27(1). RIGHT RELATIONSHIPS with other people, especially those closest to us.

9(2), 16, 25. Praying ACCORDING TO GOD'S WILL, revealed in His Word.

10(2), 12, 16(2), 27(2). APPROPRIATING BY FAITH the answer to our prayer at the actual moment that we pray. "NOW is the accepted time" (2 Cor. 6:2).

17, 18, 19. REGULARITY and PERSISTENCE (Compare Luke 18:1).

3, 11, 21, 26. FERVENCY, SELFDENIAL, COMMITMENT.

20. In all this, we cannot rely merely upon our own will, understanding or strength, but we must have the SUPERNATURAL HELP OF THE HOLY SPIRIT.

22, 28. The REWARDS for right praying.

STUDY NO. 9

WATER BAPTISM: HOW? WHEN? WHY?

Introduction

Jesus Himself said: "He that believeth and is baptised shall be saved" (Mark 16:16). God's way of salvation is still the same: first believe, then be baptised. Believing in Christ produces an inward change in our hearts; being baptised in water is an outward act of obedience, by which we testify of the change that has taken place in our hearts. By this act, we make ourselves one with Christ in His burial and in His resurrection; we are separated from the old life of sin and defeat; we come out of the water to lead a new life of righteousness and victory, made possible by God's power in us. The scriptures in this study explain very carefully how, when, and why we must be baptised.

Memory work: Romans 6:4   Please check when Memory card prepared ☐

(Review previous verse daily)

1. What reason did Jesus Himself give for being baptised? (Matt. 3:15)

   ....

   ....

2. How did the Holy Spirit show that He was pleased with the baptism of Jesus? (Matt. 3:16)

   ....

   ....

3. What did God the Father say about Jesus when He was baptised? (Matt. 3:17)

   ....

   ....

4. Did Jesus go down into the water to be baptised? (Matt. 3:16)

   ....

5. If a person wishes to be saved, what did Jesus say he should do after believing the gospel? (Mark 16:16)

   ....

6. What did Jesus tell His disciples to do to people before baptising them? (Matt. 28:19)

   ....

7. To whom did Jesus send his disciples with this message? (Matt. 28:19)

   ....

8. What does Jesus expect people to do after being baptised? (Matt. 28:20)

   ....

   ....

9. What did Peter tell people to do before being baptised? (Acts 2:38)

   ....

10. How many people did Peter say should be baptised? (Acts 2:38)

   ....

11. How did the people act who gladly received God's Word? (Acts 2:41)

....

12. What did the people of Samaria do after they believed Philip's preaching? (Acts 8:12)

....

13. What did Philip tell the eunuch he must do before he could be baptised? (Acts 8:37)

....

14. What did the eunuch answer? (Acts 8:37)

....

....

15. Did the eunuch go down into the water to be baptised? (Acts 8:38)

....

16. How did the eunuch feel after being baptised? (Acts 8:39)

....

17. After Cornelius and his friends had been saved and had received the Holy Spirit, what did Peter command them to do next? (Acts 10:44-48)

....

18. What did the Philippian jailor and his family do after believing Paul's message? (Acts 16:29-33)

....

19. What did the disciples at Ephesus do after believing Paul's message? (Acts 19:4, 5)

....

20. Through which two experiences do believers follow Christ when they are baptised? (Rom. 6:4 Col. 2:12)

(1) .... (2) ....

21. How does Paul say believers should live after being baptised? (Rom. 6:4)

....

22. Is there any difference between believers of different races after being baptised? (Gal. 3:26-28)

....

23. Mention two pictures of water baptism found in the Old Testament and referred to in the New Testament:

(a) (1 Cor.10:1, 2 Ex. 14:21, 22) ....

....

(b) (1 Pet. 3:20, 21 Gen. chs. 6 & 7) ....

....

Memory work: Romans 6:4

Write out this verse from memory.

....

....

....

....

....

DO NOT TURN THIS PAGE UNTIL YOU HAVE COMPLETED ALL ANSWERS IN THIS STUDY

STUDY NO. 9: WATER BAPTISM: HOW? WHEN? WHY?

CORRECT ANSWERS AND MARKS

Question No.	Answers	Marks
1.	"Thus it becometh us to fulfil all righteousness"	2
2.	He descended like a dove, and lighted upon Him	2
3.	"This is my beloved Son, in whom I am well pleased"	2
4.	Yes	1
5.	He should be baptised	1
6.	To teach them	1
7.	To all nations	1
8.	To observe all things which He has commanded	2
9.	To repent	1
10.	Every one	1
11.	They were baptised	1
12.	They were baptised	1
13.	Believe with all his heart	1
14.	"I believe that Jesus Christ is the Son of God"	1
15.	Yes	1
16.	He went on his way rejoicing	1
17.	To be baptised	1
18.	They were all baptised	1
19.	They were baptised	1
20.	(1) His burial (2) His resurrection	2
21.	They should walk in newness of life	2
22.	None	1
23.	(a) The Israelites passing through the Red Sea	2
	(b) Noah and his family passing through the flood in the Ark	2

Consult Bible for Written Memory Work

If word perfect, 4 marks	4
(1 mark off for each mistake. If	—
more than 3 mistakes, no marks)	TOTAL 36

50% — 18   70% — 25   80% — 29

STUDY NO. 9: WATER BAPTISM: HOW? WHEN? WHY?

NOTES ON CORRECT ANSWERS

(The numbers in the lefthand margin correspond to the numbers of the correct answers on the previous page)

1-4. Although Jesus was baptised by John the Baptist, He was not in the same class as all the others whom John baptised. John's baptism was a "baptism of repentance", accompanied by confession of sins (Mark 1:4-5). But Jesus had no sins to confess, or repent of. Rather, by being baptised in this way, Jesus set a pattern for all who would afterward follow Him in obedience to the will of God. This is indicated by the reason which Jesus gave: "Thus it becometh us to fulfil all righteousness."

"Thus" establishes the manner of baptism: going down into, and coming up out of, the water. "It becometh us" establishes a precedent, which it becomes all sincere Christians to follow. "To fulfil all righteousness" establishes the reason: to complete all righteousness. First, the Christian is made righteous through his faith in Christ. Then, in being baptised, he completes this inward righteousness of faith by the outward act of obedience. Thus understood, this ordinance of Christian baptism has the openly expressed approval of all 3 Persons of the Godhead: Father, Son and Spirit. (For a full study of this subject, see chapter 2 of my book, "From Jordan To Pentecost".)

5, 6, 9, 13. Before being baptised, a person should fulfil the following 3 conditions: (1) be taught the nature and the reason of the act; (2) repent of his sins; (3) believe in Jesus Christ as the Son of God.

7, 10, 11, 12, 17, 18, 19. Jesus told His disciples that this ordinance of baptism was to be for "all nations". There were to be no exceptions. In fulfilment of this, the New Testament record shows that all new converts were always baptised without delay. In most cases this took place on the actual day of conversion. Never was there any lengthy delay between conversion and baptism. There is no reason why this pattern should not be followed now, just as much as in the early church.

8, 20, 21. By baptism Christians publicly identify themselves with Christ in His burial and resurrection. After baptism, they are required to lead a new life of righteousness, made possible by the grace and power of the Holy Spirit.

23(a). 1 Cor. 10:1-2 presents a double baptism for God's people, "in the cloud and in the sea". Baptism "in the cloud" typifies baptism in the Holy Spirit. Baptism "in the sea" typifies baptism in water.

23(b). By faith Noah and his family entered into the ark (= Christ). Then, in the ark, they passed through the water of the flood (= baptism). They were thus saved from God's judgment, separated from the old, ungodly world, and ushered into a completely new life.

STUDY NO. 10

WITNESSING AND WINNING SOULS

Introduction

By His atoning death on the cross Christ has made salvation possible for all men everywhere. But in order to receive salvation each person must first hear the Word of God and the testimony of Christ. God's plan is that every person who is saved should be filled with the Holy Spirit and should then use this power to witness to others of Christ, and that in this way the testimony of Christ should continually be extended further and further abroad, until it has reached the uttermost part of the earth and until all nations have heard. This is the great way in which all Christians can work together to prepare the way for the return of Christ. Christians who are faithful in witnessing will receive a reward from Christ Himself, and will have the joy of seeing in heaven the souls who have been won through their testimony. Christians who are unfaithful will have to answer to God for lost souls to whom they failed witness.

Memory work: Acts 1:8   Please check when Memory card prepared ☐

(Review previous verse daily)

1. What did Christ tell His disciples that they were to be for Him? (Acts 1:8)

....

2. How far did Christ say that the witness of His disciples was to extend? (Acts 1:8)

....

3. To whom must the witness be extended before the end of this age? (Matt. 24:14)

....

4. Of what 3 things concerning Jesus did Peter say that he and the other disciples were witnesses? (Acts 10:39-41)

   (1) ....

   (2) .... (3) ....

5. What did God tell Paul that he was to do for Christ? (Acts 22:15)

....

....

6. What did Paul continue to do from the day that he came to know Jesus? (Acts 26:22)

....

....

7. What does a true witness do by his testimony? (Prov. 14:25)

....

8. What should a wise Christian seek to do? (Prov. 11:30)

....

9. After Andrew found Jesus, whom did he in turn bring to Jesus? (John 1:35-42)

....

10. After Jesus found Philip, whom did Philip in turn bring to Jesus? (John 1:43-47)

....

11. When the Pharisees questioned the man born blind, what did he answer from his own experience? (John 9:25)

....

12. What 2 things should we talk about and make known to other people? (1 Chron. 16:8, 9)

(1) .... (2) ....

13. When people opposed Paul's testimony in Corinth, what did God tell Paul? (Acts 18:9)

....

14. What spirit did Paul tell Timothy was not from God? (2 Tim. 1:7)

....

15. What does the fear of man bring? (Prov. 29:25) ....

16. What instruction did Paul give Timothy concerning the testimony of Christ? (2 Tim. 1:8)

....

17. When Peter and John were commanded not to speak about Jesus, what 2 answers did they give?

(1) (Acts 4:20) ....

(2) (Acts 5:29) ....

18. When the other disciples heard that Peter and John had been forbidden to speak about Jesus, what did they all do? (Acts 4:24)

....

19. After the disciples had prayed and been filled with the Holy Ghost, what did they all do? (Acts 4:31)

....

20. What special position did God give Ezekiel among his people? (Ezek. 3:17)

....

21. What did God tell Ezekiel would happen to him if he failed to warn the sinners? (Ezek. 3:18)

....

22. What 2 things did Paul testify to all men at Ephesus? (Acts 20:21)

(1) ....

(2) ....

23. Why could Paul say he was pure from the blood of all men at Ephesus? (Acts 20:26, 27)

....

24. What is the final reward laid up for all faithful witnesses of Christ? (2 Tim. 4:8)

....

Memory work: Acts 1:8

Write out this verse from memory.

....

....

....

....

....

DO NOT TURN THIS PAGE UNTIL YOU HAVE COMPLETED ALL ANSWERS IN THIS STUDY

STUDY NO. 10: WITNESSING AND WINNING SOULS

CORRECT ANSWERS AND MARKS

Question No.	Answers	Marks
1.	Witnesses	1
2.	To the uttermost part of the earth	1
3.	To all nations	1
4.	(1) All that he did	1
	(2) His death (3) His resurrection	2
5.	To be his witness to all men of what he had seen and heard	3
6.	Witnessing both to small and great that the scriptures were true	3
7.	He delivers souls	1
8.	To win souls	1
9.	His brother, Simon Peter	1
10.	Nathanael	1
11.	"One thing I know, that, whereas I was blind, now I see"	2
12.	(1) God's deeds (2) His wondrous works	2
13.	"Be not afraid, but speak"	2
14.	The spirit of fear	1
15.	A snare	1
16.	Not to be ashamed of the testimony of Christ	2
17.	(1) "We cannot but speak the things which we have seen and heard"	2
	(2) "We ought to obey God rather than men"	1
18.	They all prayed to God with one accord	2
19.	They spoke the word of God with boldness	1
20.	A watchman	1
21.	God would require their blood at his hand	2
22.	(1) Repentance toward God	1
	(2) Faith toward our Lord Jesus Christ	1
23.	Because he had not shunned to declare unto them all the counsel of God	2
24.	A crown of righteousness	1

Consult Bible for Written Memory Work

If word perfect, 4 marks 4
(1 mark off for each mistake. If —
more than 3 mistakes, no marks)   TOTAL 44

50% — 22   70% — 31   80% — 35

STUDY NO. 10: WITNESSING AND WINNING SOULS

NOTES ON CORRECT ANSWERS

(The numbers in the lefthand margin correspond to the numbers of the correct answers on the previous page)

1. Christians are not intended to be witnesses primarily to a doctrine, an experience, or a denomination, but to CHRIST HIMSELF. Jesus said: "I, if I be lifted up from the earth, will draw all men unto me" (John 12:32). Christian testimony should uplift Jesus. To do this effectively, it must be directed and empowered by the Holy Spirit.

4. Compare Acts 1:21-22 and 4:33. The central fact of all testimony concerning Christ is His RESURRECTION from the dead.

5-6. Paul's testimony is a pattern for all Christians. It was based on personal experience; it pointed to Christ; it confirmed the record of the scriptures.

7-8. Faithful personal testimony is the most effective way to win other souls to Christ.

9-10. Although Peter later became the acknowledged leader among the apostles and the chief preacher, it was his brother Andrew who first came to Christ, and then brought Peter in turn. Later, Philip in the same way brought Nathanael. Thus the pattern of individual soul-winning is set by the apostles themselves.

11. Someone has said: "The man with an experience is not at the mercy of the man with an argument."

12. A Christian's conversation should be positive, glorifying God, and building his own faith and that of others.

13-16, 19. The greatest hindrance to effective Christian testimony is "the spirit of fear" (timidity). The Bible teaches clearly that this spirit does not come from God, and that a Christian should not allow himself to be ensnared or bound by it. The remedy is to be filled with the Holy Spirit.

17(2). Where there is a clear cut choice between obedience to God and obedience to man, this answer of Peter and John is just as valid today.

18. Prayer is the great weapon given to Christians to break down the barriers to their testimony.

20-23. Like Ezekiel in the Old Testament, Paul in the New Testament understood that he would be held accountable by God for those to whom he had been given opportunity to testify. He understood also that he was required by God to "keep back nothing", but to declare "all the counsel of God". God still requires the same of Christians today.

STUDY NO. 11

GOD'S PLAN FOR PROSPERITY

Introduction

All through the Bible God promises to bless and prosper those who trust and serve Him. In order to receive God's financial and material blessings, we must learn to follow God's rule of faith, which says: "Give, and it shall be given unto you" (Luke 6:38). We begin by giving back to God the first tenth of all that we receive, in money or in produce. This first tenth, set aside for God, is called our "tithe". Over and above this "tithe", we bring our "offerings" to God, as the Holy Spirit directs us. As we do this in faith, God abundantly blesses us and supplies all our needs.

Memory work: Matt. 6:33   Please check when Memory card prepared ☐

(Review previous verse daily)

A. EXAMPLES OF GOD'S SERVANTS WHO HAVE PROSPERED

1. When God gave Abraham victory in battle, what did Abraham give back to God's priest, Melchizedek? (Gen. 14:19-20)

....

2. How did God in turn deal with Abraham? (Gen. 24:1)

....

3. What 3 things did Jacob want God to do for him? (Gen. 28:20)

   (1) ....

   (2)..

   (3) ....

4. What did Jacob promise to give God in return? (Gen. 28:22)

....

5. How did God in turn deal with Jacob? (Gen. 33:11)

....

6. What kind of man was Joseph? (Gen. 39:2)

....

7. What was the reason of Joseph's prosperity? (Gen. 39:2, 23)

....

8. What 3 things did God command Joshua concerning His law? (Josh. 1:8)

   (1) ....

   (2) ....

   (3) ....

9. What did God promise Joshua if he would do these 3 things? (Josh. 1:8)

....

10. What did David promise Solomon if he would obey all the statutes and judgments of God's law? (1 Chron. 22:13)

....

11. As long as Uzziah sought the Lord, what did God do for him? (2 Chron. 26:5)

....

12. When Hezekiah sought and served God with all his heart, what happened to him? (2 Chron. 31:21 and 32:30)

....

B. CONDITIONS AND PROMISES OF PROSPERITY

13. Concerning a certain kind of person, God says that "whatsoever he doeth shall prosper" (Psa. 1:3)

    (a) Write down 3 things that such a person must NOT do (Psa. 1:1)

    (1) ....

    (2) ....

    (3) ....

    (b) Write down 2 things that such a person MUST do (Psa. 1:2)

    (1) ....

    (2) ....

14. In what 2 ways did God say that Israel had been robbing Him? (Mal. 3:8)

    (1) .... (2) ....

15. What happened to Israel as a result of robbing God? (Mal. 3:9)

    ....

16. How did God tell Israel to "prove" Him (i.e. put Him to the test)? (Mal. 3:10)

    ....

17. What did God promise Israel that He would then do for them? (Mal. 3:10)

    ....

18. What 2 things does Christ tell Christians to seek before all others? (Matt. 6:33)

    (1) .... (2) ....

19. What result does Christ promise will then follow? (Matt. 6:33)

    ....

20. When we give, with what measure will it be given back to us? (Luke 6:38)

    ....

21. By what standard did Paul tell each Christian to measure how much he should set aside for God? (1 Cor. 16:2)

    ....

22. For what purpose did Christ become poor? (2 Cor. 8:9)

    ....

23. What kind of person does God love? (2 Cor. 9:7)

    ....

24. If we wish to reap bountifully, what must we do first? (2 Cor. 9:6)

    ....

25. If God's grace abounds towards us, what 2 results will follow? (2 Cor. 9:8)

    (1) ....

    (2) ....

26. From what kind of people will God withhold no good thing? (Psa. 84:11)

    ....

27. What kind of people will not want (lack) any good thing ? (Psa. 34:10)

    ....

28. In what does the Lord take pleasure? (Psa. 35:27)

    ....

Memory work: Matt. 6:33

Write out this verse from memory.

....

....

....

....

DO NOT TURN THIS PAGE UNTIL YOU HAVE COMPLETED ALL ANSWERS IN THIS STUDY

STUDY NO. 11: GOD'S PLAN FOR PROSPERITY

CORRECT ANSWERS AND MARKS

Question No.	Answers	Marks
1.	Tithes of all	1
2.	God blessed Abraham in all things	1
3.	(1) Be with him	1
	(2) Keep him in the way that he went	1
	(3) Give him bread to eat and raiment to put on	1
4.	A tenth of all that God would give him	1
5.	God dealt graciously with Jacob	1
6.	A prosperous man	1
7.	The Lord was with him and made what he did to prosper	2
8.	(1) It should not depart out of his mouth	1
	(2) He should meditate in it day and night	1
	(3) He should observe to do everything that was written in it	1
9.	He would make his way prosperous and have good success	2
10.	Then shalt thou prosper	1
11.	God made him to prosper	1
12.	He prospered in all his works	1
13.	(a) (1) NOT walk in the counsel of the ungodly	1
	(2) NOT stand in the way of sinners	1
	(3) NOT sit in the seat of the scornful	1
	(b) (1) He MUST delight in the law of the Lord	1
	(2) He MUST meditate in it day and night	1
14.	(1) In tithes (2) In offerings	2
15.	The whole nation was cursed with a curse	1
16.	By bringing all the tithes into the storehouse	1
17.	Open the windows of heaven and pour out such a blessing that there would not be room to contain it	2
18.	(1) The kingdom of God (2) The righteousness of God	2
19.	All the material things that they need will be added to them	1
20.	With the same measure that we "mete" (= measure) with	1
21.	As God hath prospered him	1
22.	That we through His poverty might be rich	1
23.	A cheerful giver	1
24.	We must sow bountifully	1
25.	(1) We shall always have all sufficiency in all things	1
	(2) We shall abound to every good work	1
26.	Them that walk uprightly	1
27.	They that seek the Lord	1
28.	In the prosperity of His servant	1

Consult Bible for Written Memory Work

If word perfect, 4 marks 4
(I mark off for each mistake. If   —
more than 3 mistakes, no marks)   **TOTAL 46**

50% — 23   70% — 32   80% — 37

—48—

STUDY NO. 11: GOD'S PLAN FOR PROSPERITY

NOTES ON CORRECT ANSWERS

(The numbers in the lefthand margin correspond to the numbers of the correct answers on the previous page)

1-5. Note that the practice of "tithing" did not begin with the law of Moses. The first person recorded in the Bible as giving tithes is Abraham. In Rom. 4:11-12 Abraham is called "the father of all them that believe ... who also walk in the steps of that faith of our father Abraham." Believers who give their tithes to God today are certainly "walking in the steps of the faith of Abraham." Note also that the priest to whom Abraham gave tithes was Melchizedek. In Heb. chs. 5, 6, 7, it is shown that Christ is our great "High Priest after the order of Melchizedek." In this capacity, He still receives the tithes of His believing people.

Both Abraham and Jacob experienced God's material blessings as a result of their tithing. In Gen. 32:10 Jacob says: "With my staff I passed over Jordan, and now I am become two bands." When Jacob started to give tithes to God, he owned nothing but the staff in his hand. Twenty years later he was the prosperous head of a large and flourishing household.

6-7. Outward circumstances cannot prevent God from keeping His promises. Even in the prison Joseph prospered. Much more so, when he became prime minister of Egypt. Joseph's prosperity was the outworking of his character and his relationship to God.

8-9. Joshua was called to lead God's people into "the promised land". Today Christians are called to enter "a land of promises". Then or now, the conditions for success are the same. Note especially the importance of right meditation. Compare the answer to question 13(b)(2).

10-12. From David to the Babylonian captivity, God prospered every king of Judah who was obedient to the law and faithful in the service of the temple.

13. Note that Psa. 1:1-3 does not describe one particuar historical character, but applies generally to every believer who fulfils the conditions stated.

14-15. Unfaithfulness by God's people in giving to God can bring a national curse. This principle still applies today.

16-21. The only basis of righteousness acceptable to God is FAITH. "Whatsoever is not of faith is sin" (Rom. 14:23). Compare Heb. 11:6. This principle applies in our financial dealings as much as in every other part of our life.

22. According to the Bible, poverty is a curse. Deut. 28:15-68 lists all the curses that result from breaking God's law. In verse 48 the following are included: "Thou shalt serve thine enemies ... in hunger ... in thirst ... in nakedness ... in want of all things." This is absolute poverty. On the cross Christ took upon Himself every one of these curses (See Gal. 3:13-14). He was hungry, thirsty, naked, in want of all things. He did this that believers might in return receive God's abundant provision for every need (See Phil. 4:19).

23. "Cheerful"; literally, "hilarious".

24. Christians should give in the same way that a farmer sows seed — carefully, intelligently, in the area calculated to yield the best returns for God's kingdom.

26-28. Prosperity is God's will for His believing, obedient people.

STUDY NO. 12

THE SECOND COMING OF CHRIST

Introduction

When Jesus Christ first came to earth about 1900 years ago, His coming exactly fulfilled in every detail all the prophecies of the Bible relating to that event. When He left this earth to return to heaven, He promised His disciples very definitely that He would come back to the earth again. Apart from these promises which Jesus Himself gave, there are many prophecies throughout the whole Bible concerning the second coming of Christ — even more, in fact, than there are about His first coming. Since the prophecies of His first coming were exactly and literally fulfilled, it is reasonable to believe that the prophecies of His second coming will be fulfilled in the same way. The scriptures in this study contain the clear promises of Christ's return. They also tell us what will happen to Christians at that time, and how Christians must in the meanwhile prepare themselves.

Memory work: Luke 21:36   Please check when Memory card prepared ☐

(Review previous verse daily)

A. PROMISES OF CHRIST'S RETURN

1. For what purpose did Christ say He was leaving His disciples? (John 14:2)

   ....

2. What promise did Christ give His disciples when He left them? (John 14:3)

   ....

3. When Christ was taken up into heaven, what promise did the angels give? (Acts 1:11)

   ....

   ....

4. What is the "blessed hope" to which all true Christians look forward? (Tit. 2:13)

   ....

5. What 3 sounds will be heard when Christ descends from heaven? (1 Thes. 4:16)

   (1) .... (2) ....

   (3) ....

B. WHAT WILL HAPPEN TO CHRISTIANS

6. Will all Christians have died when Christ comes? (1 Cor. 15:51)

   ....

7. At this time what will happen to Christians who have died? (1 Thes. 4:16)

   ....

8. Write down 2 things that will then happen to all Christians, whether they have died or not.

   (1) (1 Cor. 15:51) ....

   ....

   (2) (1 Thes. 4:17) ....

   ....

9. Will these Christians ever again be separated from the Lord? (1 Thes. 4:17)

   ....

10. When we actually see the Lord, what change will take place in us? (1 John 3:2)

....

11. As a result of this change, what will the body of the Christian then be like? (Phil. 3:21)

....

12. What 2 words does Paul use to describe the body of the Christian after resurrection? (1 Cor. 15:53)

(1) .... (2) ....

13. How does the Bible describe the feast which Christians will then enjoy? (Rev. 19:9)

....

C. HOW CHRISTIANS MUST PREPARE

14. What did the Lamb's wife do before the marriage supper? (Rev. 19:7)

....

15. What kind of clothing did she wear? (Rev. 19:8)

....

16. What does the fine linen represent? (Rev. 19:8)

....

17. Of the 10 virgins, which ones went in to the marriage? (Matt. 25:10)

....

18. If a man has the hope of seeing the Lord when He comes, how does he prepare himself for this? (1 John 3:3)

....

19. To whom will Christ appear the second time unto salvation? (Heb. 9:28)

....

20. What 2 things must we follow after, if we desire to see the Lord? (Heb. 12:14)

(1) .... (2) ....

21. Write down 3 conditions which should mark out all Christians at Christ's coming (2 Pet. 3:14)

(1) .... (2) .... (3) ....

23. What expression does Christ use to show how sudden His coming will be? (Rev. 3:3; 16:15)

....

23. Who knows the day and hour of Christ's coming? (Mark 13:32)

....

24. What did Christ warn all Christians to do in view of His coming? (Mark 13:35-37)

....

25. What did Christ warn Christians to do in addition to watching? (Luke 21:36)

....

26. What 3 things did Christ warn Christians could keep them from being ready? (Luke 21:34)

(1) .... (2) .... (3) ....

Memory work: Luke 21:36

Write out this verse from memory

....
....
....
....

DO NOT TURN THIS PAGE UNTIL YOU HAVE COMPLETED ALL ANSWERS IN THIS STUDY

STUDY NO. 12: THE SECOND COMING OF CHRIST

CORRECT ANSWERS AND MARKS

Question No.	Answers	Marks
1.	To go and prepare a place for them	1
2.	I will come again and receive you unto myself	2
3.	This same Jesus shall so come in like manner as ye have seen him go into heaven	2
4.	The glorious appearing of the great God and our Saviour Jesus Christ	2
5.	(1) A shout (2) The voice of the archangel	2
	(3) The trump of God	1
6.	No.	1
7.	They will arise (from the dead)	1
8.	(1) They will all be changed	1
	(2) They will all be caught up in the clouds to meet the Lord in the air	2
9.	Never	1
10.	We shall be like him	1
11.	Like the glorious (glorified) body of Christ	1
12.	(1) Incorruption (2) Immortality	2
13.	The marriage supper of the Lamb (Christ)	1
14.	She made herself ready	1
15.	Fine linen, clean and white (bright)	1
16.	The righteousness of saints	1
17.	They that were ready	1
18.	He purifies himself even as he (Christ) is pure	2
19.	To them that look for him	1
20.	(1) Peace with all men (2) Holiness	2
21.	(1) In peace (2) Without spot (3) Blameless	3
22.	"As a thief"	1
23.	Only God the Father	1
24.	To watch	1
25.	To pray always	1
26.	(1) Surfeiting (Gluttony) (2) Drunkenness	2
	(3) Cares of this life	1

Consult Bible for Written Memory Work

If word perfect, 4 marks 4
(I mark off for each mistake. If   —
more than 3 mistakes, no marks)   TOTAL 44

50% — 22   70% — 31   80% — 35

STUDY NO. 12: THE SECOND COMING OF CHRIST

NOTES ON CORRECT ANSWERS

(The numbers in the lefthand margin correspond to the numbers of the correct answers on the previous page)

1-5. "Out of the mouth of 2 or 3 witnesses shall every word be established" (Matt. 18:16, etc.). Concerning the return of Christ we have the 3 witnesses: (1) Christ Himself (John 14:3); (2) the angels (Acts 1:11); (3) the apostle Paul (1 Thes. 4:16). Note the emphasis on the return of Christ IN PERSON: "THIS SAME Jesus ..." "The Lord HIMSELF ..." This "blessed hope" is the supreme goal of all Christian living.

5.(1) The "shout" will come from the Lord Himself, for His voice alone has power to call forth the dead (See John 5:28-29). (2) The archangel will presumably be Gabriel, whose special duty is to announce impending interventions of God in the affairs of men (See Luke 1:19, 26). (3) The trumpet is used to call God's people together (Num. 10:2-3).

6. To "sleep" means to "die" (Compare Acts 7:60 1 Cor. 11:30). This word is particularly used of the death of Christians, because they look forward to "waking" again on the resurrection morning.

6-8. The following order of events is indicated: (1) Dead Christians will be resurrected with new, glorified bodies. (2) Living Christians will have their bodies instantaneously changed to similar, glorified bodies. (3) All Christians will be caught up together in clouds to meet the Lord as He descends from heaven.

10-12. The glorified body of the Christian will be like the Lord's own glorified body. (For a fuller study of this subject, see chapter 8 of my book, "Resurrection Of The Dead".)

13. Compare Matt. 8:11; 26:29.

14-21, 24-25. The Bible very clearly teaches that, in order to be ready for the return of Christ, Christians will have to prepare themselves diligently. In Rev. 19:8 the literal translation is "the righteousnesses—or righteous acts —of saints". This is the outworking in practical Christian living of the righteousness of Christ received by faith. Compare Phil. 2:12-13: "Work out ... for it is God that worketh in you." The main requirements of God's Word in this respect may be summarised as follows: (1) Purity (without spot) (1 John 3:3 2 Pet. 3:14); (2) Holiness (Heb. 12:14); (3) Peacec (= right relations with all men (Heb. 12:14 2 Pet. 3:14); (4) Blamelessness (= faithfulness in all Christian duties) (2 Pet. 3:14); (5) Expectancy (Heb. 9:28); (6) Watchfulness (Mark 13:37); (7) Prayerfulness (Luke 21:36).

22. Christ will be "like a thief" in the manner of His coming, but He will take only that which is His own. It is "they that are Christ's at His coming" (1 Cor. 15:23).

23. When the moment comes, the Father will tell the Son. Then all heaven will be stirred to action.

26. (1) Christ always warned against "gluttony" before "drunkenness".

(3) Compare Luke 17:27-28. The things mentioned here are not sinful in themselves. The sin consists in becoming absorbed in them.

SIGNS OF CHRIST'S COMING

Introduction

The Bible tells us of various special things which will be happening in the world at the time just before Christ's second coming, and which will be signs to warn us that He is coming soon. In this study some of the most important signs are stated. They are divided into two groups: A. SIGNS IN THE WORLD OF RELIGION; B. SIGNS IN THE WORLD AT LARGE. Below each group of signs are given the references to the passages of scripture in which those signs are mentioned.

In this study you are required to do the following:-

(1) Read through the signs in Group A.

(2) Read through the scriptures of which the references are given below Group A.

(3) On the dotted line below each sign, write in the reference of the scripture which mentions that sign.

(4) Repeat the same procedure for Group B.

(5) At the end of each sign you will see a square "box" (☐). When you have done the rest of the study, read through the signs once again, and check each "box" if you feel that that particular sign is being fulfilled in the world as you know it today.

(NOTE: There is one appropriate scripture reference for each sign. However, Matt. 24:9 applies to three different signs, and must be written in after each sign to which it applies.)

Memory work: Luke 21:28   Please check when Memory card prepared ☐

(Review previous pages daily)

A. SIGNS IN THE WORLD OF RELIGION

1. Worldwide outpouring of the Holy Spirit   ☐

....

2. Worldwide evangelism and missionary activity   ☐

....

3. Christians afflicted, killed and hated   ☐

....

4. Many false prophets   ☐

....

5. A great falling away from the Christian faith   ☐

....

6. Many Christians being led astray by deceptions of the devil   ☐

....

7. The love of many Christians growing cold   ☐

....

SCRIPTURE REFERENCES

Matt. 24:12	1 Tim. 4:1	Matt. 24:9	Acts 2:17	Matt. 24:11
2 Thes. 2:3	Matt. 24:14			

B. SIGNS IN THE WORLD AT LARGE

8. Great international wars ☐

....

9. Increase of travel and knowledge ☐

....

10. Rise of Zionism and rebuilding of the State of Israel ☐

....

11. Jerusalem liberated from Gentile dominion ☐

....

12. Many scoffers, denying the Word of God and the promise of Christ's return ☐

....

13. People absorbed in material pleasures and pursuits, and forgetting the impending judgments of God ☐

....

14. Great decline in moral and ethical standards, combined with the outward forms of religion ☐

....

15. Abounding iniquity (literally, "lawlessness") ☐

....

16. Famines and pestilences ☐

....

17. Increase in severity and frequency of earthquakes ☐

....

18. Distress and perplexity of nations ☐

....

19. Many anti-christs ☐

....

SCRIPTURE REFERENCES

Matt. 24:12	Luke 21:24	1 John 2:18	2 Pet. 3:2-7	Dan. 12:4
Matt. 24:7	Luke 17:26-30	Psa. 102:16	2 Tim. 3:1-5	Luke 21:25

DO NOT TURN THIS PAGE UNTIL YOU HAVE COMPLETED ALL ANSWERS IN THIS STUDY

STUDY NO. 13: SIGNS OF CHRIST'S COMING

CORRECT ANSWERS AND MARKS

Question No.	Answers	Marks
1. Acts 2:17		1
2. Matt. 24:14		1
3. Matt. 24:9		1
4. Matt. 24:11		1
5. 2 Thes. 2:3		1
6. 1 Tim. 4:1		1
7. Matt. 24:12		1
8. Matt. 24:7		1
9. Dan. 12:4		1
10. Psa. 102:16		1
11. Luke 21:24		1
12. 2 Pet. 3:2-7		1
13. Luke 17:26-30		1
14. 2 Tim. 3:1-5		1
15. Matt. 24:12		1
16. Matt. 24:7		1
17. Matt. 24:7		1
18. Luke 21:25		1
19. 1 John 2:18		1

Consult Bible for Written Memory Work

If word perfect, 4 marks 4
(1 mark off for each mistake. If —
more than 3 mistakes, no marks) TOTAL 23

50% — 11   70% — 16   80% — 18

THREE FINAL IMPORTANT QUESTIONS

There are nineteen different signs of Christ's coming mentioned in this study.

Against HOW MANY of them did YOU place a CHECK?

....

Does this indicate to you that Christ may be coming SOON?

....

If so, are you READY?

....

STUDY NO. 13: SIGNS OF CHRIST'S COMING

NOTES ON CORRECT ANSWERS

(The numbers in the lefthand margin correspond to the numbers of the correct answers on the previous page)

1. The expression "all flesh" denotes the entire human race. It is often used with this meaning in the prophets. See Is. 40:5, 6 Jer. 25:31 Ezek. 21:4, 5. Every section of the human race will feel the impact of this last great outpouring of God's Spirit.

2. Evangelistic and missionary outreach are the natural outcome of the outpouring of God's Spirit. Note the special comment after this sign: "And then shall the end come."

3. It is estimated that there have been more Christian martyrs in this century than in any preceding century. Under atheistic communism, amongst one third of the world's population, Christianity is systematically persecuted.

4-6. These 3 signs all indicate a tremendous increase towards the close of this age in Satanic pressures and deceptions aimed at seducing Christians from their loyalty to Christ. The Bible indicates that at the end there will be only 2 significant groups within Christendom, the one described as a "bride", and the other as a "harlot". The "bride" is identified by her faithfulness to the "bridegroom" (= Christ). Conversely, the "harlot" is identified by her unfaithfulness to Christ. See Rev. chs. 17 and 18.

7. This sign corresponds with the picture of Laodicea, the last of the 7 churches of Revelation, whose damning sin is "lukewarmness" (Rev. 3:14-22). This decline in the love of Christians will be mainly due to one or more of the following factors: (1) bitter persecution; (2) Satanic deception; (3) prevailing materialism.

8. This century has seen wars greater and more numerous than any preceding century, especially the 2 "World Wars".

9. Note how these 2 factors are logically connected. The increase in knowledge (science) has made possible the increase in travel. Likewise, the icrease in travel contributes to the increase of knowledge.

10-11. The rise of Zionism, the rebirth of the State of Israel, and the "six-day war" of 1967 are among the great miracles of modern history. Someone has said: "The Jews are the minute hand on God's prophetic clock, and that hand has almost reached midnight."

12. The past century has witnessed systematic attacks on the Bible such as no previous century can record. Paradoxically enough, these attacks on the Bible are actually confirmations of its accuracy, since the Bible clearly predicts them.

13-15, 18. These signs are attested daily by the newspapers of the modern world. Compare Luke 17:26 with Gen. 6:5, 12, 13. The three main evil features of Noah's day were: (1) evil imaginations; (2) sexual corruption and perversion; (3) violence.

16. Famines and pestilences naturally tend to go together, and both are often caused by war.

17. Records over the past century indicate a marked increase of earthquakes.

19. The work of "the spirit of anti-christ" is twofold: first, to displace Christ from His God-given position of authority and supremacy; second, to raise up another in Christ's place. In this sense, the 3 main political "isms" of this generation — Fascism, Nazism and Communism — have all been "anti-christian" (as are many other political and religious forces at work in the world today). However, the world still awaits the final "anti-christ", as described in 2 Thes. 2:3-12, etc.

STUDY NO. 14

REVIEW

Introduction

The purpose of this last study is to fix firmly in your mind the many important truths which you have learned from the previous studies. Review is an essential part of all thorough learning. If you are willing to work steadily through this last study, carefully following the instructions step by step, you will greatly increase the benefit and blessing which you have received from the previous studies, and you will find out for yourself just how much you have really learned. Do not omit the review of the Memory work!

Final Memory work: James 1:25

Please check when Memory card prepared ☐

(Review previous verse daily)

First, read carefully through all the questions of the previous 13 studies, together with the corresponding correct answers. Check that you now know and understand the correct answer to each question.

Secondly, review all the passages which you have learned for Memory work.

Thirdly, write the answers to Sections A and B below.

SECTION A: Write below, in the spaces provided, 4 Important Truths from the Bible, which you have learned from this course. In each case, write down the references to the passages in the Bible where that truth is found.

First truth..

....

....

....

....

....

Bible References:...

....

Second truth...

....

....

....

....

....

Bible References:...

....

Third truth ....
....
....
....
....

Bible References: ....
....

Fourth truth ....
....
....
....
....

Bible References: ....
....

SECTION B. In the space below, describe briefly any important changes which have taken place in your own life through studying the Bible.

....
....
....
....
....
....
....
....
....
....

NOTE: There are no marks allotted for Sections A and B above.

Final Memory work : James 1:25

Write out this verse from memory.

....
....
....
....

Marks for the above Memory Work:

If word perfect, 4 marks 4
(1 mark off for each mistake. If   —
more than 3 mistakes, no marks.)   TOTAL MARKS FOR THIS STUDY 4

MARKS FOR THE COURSE

How to assess your own results:

Write your marks for each study in the space provided below in the right-hand column. Add up your own total, and compare it with the standards given for Pass, Credit or Distinction.

STUDY NO. 1	....	54	....
STUDY NO. 2	....	40	....
STUDY NO. 3	....	40	....
STUDY NO. 4	....	44	....
STUDY NO. 5	....	49	....
STUDY NO. 6	....	38	....
STUDY NO. 7	....	59	....
STUDY NO. 8	....	49	....
STUDY NO. 9	....	36	....
STUDY NO. 10	....	44	....
STUDY NO. 11	....	46	....
STUDY NO. 12	....	44	....
STUDY NO. 13	....	23	....
STUDY NO. 14	....	4	....

TOTAL 570

PASS	.... 50%	....	285
CREDIT	.... 70%	....	399
DISTINCTION	.... 80%	....	456

*   *   *   *   *

CONGRATULATIONS ON COMPLETING THE COURSE!

Now you will want to explore the truths of the Bible in further systematic study.

ABOUT THE AUTHOR

Derek Prince (1915–2003) was born in Bangalore, India, into a British military family. He was educated at Eton College and Cambridge University (B.A. and M.A.) in England and later at Hebrew University, Israel. As a student, he was a philosopher and self-proclaimed atheist. He was elected a fellow at King's College, Cambridge.

While in the British Medical Corps during World War II, Prince began to study the Bible as a philosophical work. Converted through a powerful encounter with Jesus Christ, he was baptized in the Holy Spirit a few days later. This life-changing experience altered the whole course of his life, which he thereafter devoted to studying and teaching the Bible as the Word of God.

At the end of World War II, he remained where the British Army had placed him—in Jerusalem. He and his family saw the rebirth of the state of Israel in 1948. In the late '50s, he served as principal of a college in Kenya.

In 1963 Prince immigrated to the United States and pastored a church in Seattle. Stirred by the tragedy of John F. Kennedy's assassination, he began to teach Americans how to intercede for their nation. In 1973 he became one of the founders of Intercessors for America. His book *Shaping History through Prayer and Fasting* has awakened Christians around the world to their responsibility to pray for their governments. Many consider underground translations of the book as instrumental in the fall of communist regimes in the USSR, East Germany, and Czechoslovakia.

Until a few years before his death at the age of 88, Prince traveled the world, imparting God's revealed truth, praying for the sick and afflicted, and sharing his prophetic insights into world events in the light of Scripture. He wrote over 45 books, which have been translated into over 60 languages and distributed worldwide. He pioneered teaching on such groundbreaking themes as generational curses, the biblical significance of Israel, and demonology.

Derek Prince Ministries, with its international headquarters in Charlotte, North Carolina, continues to distribute his teachings and to train missionaries, church leaders, and congregations through its worldwide branch offices. It is estimated that Derek Prince's clear, non-denominational, non-sectarian teaching of the Bible has reached more than half the globe through his books, tapes, and daily radio program, *Keys to Successful Living*.

Internationally recognized as a Bible scholar and spiritual patriarch, Derek Prince taught and ministered on six continents for over seven decades. In 2002 he said, "It is my desire—and I believe the Lord's desire—that this ministry continue the work, which God began through me over sixty years ago, until Jesus returns."

MORE POWERFUL TITLES BY DEREK PRINCE

Baptism in the Holy Spirit
ISBN: 0-88368-377-6 • Pocket • 80 pages

Derek Prince on Experiencing God's Power
ISBN: 0-88368-551-5 • Trade • 528 pages

Does Your Tongue Need Healing?
ISBN: 0-88368-239-7 • Pocket • 112 pages

Faith to Live By
ISBN: 0-88368-519-1 • Trade • 176 pages

Fasting
ISBN: 0-88368-258-3 • Pocket • 64 pages

God's Medicine Bottle
ISBN: 0-88368-332-6 • Pocket • 64 pages

God's Plan for Your Money
ISBN: 0-88368-707-0 • Trade • 96 pages

God's Remedy for Rejection
ISBN: 0-88368-864-6 • Trade • 112 pages

God's Will for Your Life
ISBN: 0-88368-408-X • Trade • 64 pages

The Grace of Yielding
ISBN: 0-88368-693-7 • Trade • 96 pages

The Holy Spirit in You
ISBN: 0-88368-961-8 • Trade • 112 pages

How to Fast Successfully
ISBN: 0-88368-345-8 • Pocket • 80 pages

Judging: When? Why? How?
ISBN: 0-88368-695-3 • Trade • 128 pages

The Marriage Covenant
ISBN: 0-88368-333-4 • Pocket • 128 pages

Prayers and Proclamations
ISBN: 0-88368-226-5 • Pocket • 96 pages

Receiving God's Best
ISBN: 0-88368-593-0 • Pocket • 112 pages

Shaping History through Prayer and Fasting
ISBN: 0-88368-773-9 • Trade • 192 pages

Spiritual Warfare
ISBN: 0-88368-670-8 • Trade • 144 pages

ɰ
WHITAKER
HOUSE

proclaiming the power of the Gospel through the written word
visit our website at www.whitakerhouse.com